TEACH YOURSELF BOOKS

Beginner's
SPANISH

Beginner's
SPANISH

Mark Stacey
Angela González Hevia
Advisory Editor: Paul Coggle

TEACH YOURSELF BOOKS

Long-renowned as the authoritative source for self-guided learning – with more than 30 million copies sold worldwide – the *Teach Yourself* series includes over 200 titles in the fields of languages, crafts, hobbies, sports, and other leisure activities.

British Library Cataloguing in Publication Data
Stacey, Mark
   Teach yourself beginner's Spanish: An easy introduction
   I. Title II. Hevia, Angela González
   468.07

Library of Congress Catalog Card Number: 92-80890

First published in UK 1992 by Hodder Headline Plc, 338 Euston Road, London NW1 3BH

First published in US 1992 by NTC Publishing Group, 4255 West Touhy Avenue, Lincolnwood (Chicago), Illinois 60646 – 1975 U.S.A.

The 'Teach Yourself' name and logo are registered trade marks of Hodder & Stoughton Ltd in the UK.

Printed in Great Britain by Cox & Wyman Ltd, Reading, Berkshire.

Impression number	20	19	18	17	16	15	14
Year		1999	1998	1997	1996		

CONTENTS

──INTRODUCTION──

So you want to learn Spanish. Welcome, then, to one of the world's great languages! In terms of numbers, Spanish is one of the most widely spoken tongues: as well as the nearly 40 million speakers in Spain, there are at least six times that number in other parts of the world, principally, of course, in Central and South America.

How much Spanish you wish or need to learn is a matter of personal choice or circumstance. You can acquire sufficient social and survival skills to 'get by' on holiday in Spain in a matter of a few weeks. At the other end of the spectrum, you can make the study of the language a life's work – Spanish is one of the main sources of European culture and literature.

The aim of this book, however, is modest. We aim to give you enough language ability to understand and to make yourself understood in not-too-complicated everyday situations; we aim also to give you a foundation for further study if, as we hope, you acquire a love for the language and its people and want to take your studies further. Though this book is designed to help you learn by yourself, don't forget that language is above all else a social activity: try to find every occasion to listen to Spanish and if possible to speak it, however haltingly. Spaniards greatly appreciate any effort people make in their language, of which they are proud, and are usually quite flattering about your efforts. So your confidence receives a boost and you are inspired to try further. Confidence is half the battle in learning to speak another language. Never be afraid to have a go; don't worry too much about making mistakes – the main thing is to communicate. If you are successful in getting your meaning across, then you are successful in using the language.

─────── How to use this book ───────

This course is divided into two parts, of 11 and 10 units.

Units 1–11

You must study the first 11 units in order; as you do so, you will find you are acquiring many useful language uses, but they are not grouped in any sort of topic area. They are based on what we call language *functions,* which are uses of language that can apply to a wide variety of situations.

Each of the first 11 units includes at least one dialogue or a description by a Spanish character of an aspect of their everyday life. It is important to listen to (or read) this material at least twice; work out the meaning for yourself as far as you can, but use the list of key words and phrases given below each dialogue or passage to help you.

The **Para estudiar** and **Comentario** sections in each of these units explain how the Spanish in the material you have just studied is put together and sometimes include relevant background information too. Particularly noteworthy points are highlighted by the symbol ✄ – these are often points where Spanish differs from English in unexpected ways.

The **Actividad** (*exercise*) section(s) in each unit gives you the opportunity to try out the Spanish that has been explained in the unit so far. The *Key* (Clave) is at the back of the book. If you have difficulty with an item in the **Actividades**, try solving the problem first of all by looking again at the Spanish in the dialogues or passages, before using the **Clave** as a last resort. However, do check the *Key* when you've done each exercise – it is important to go back over material in areas where you are making errors, rather than carrying on regardless, which is bound to get you into trouble later! If you find you are making a large number of errors, try taking things more slowly and practising the phrases more as you go through the material in the unit – don't try an **Actividad** until you are pretty sure you have understood everything that precedes it, as you will find that if you rush you may make less progress in the end. If you have the cassette, make good use of the pause button – it's good for your pronunciation and your memory to repeat phrases as often as possible.

Finally in each of Units 1–10, there is a short test – **Evaluación**, which enables you to check whether you can now do some of the language tasks covered by that unit. The answers to these tests are also given in the **Clave**. Always check your results in the test, and revise the unit until you can do it without errors before you go on to the next unit. A thorough understanding of everything in Unit 1 is essential for you to succeed in Unit 2, and so on.

Units 12–21

The next nine units, numbered 12 to 20, are based as you will see on broad topic areas. They can be taken in any order, which enables you to learn first how to cope with shopping, say, (Unit 17), if this is what you feel you need to tackle before anything else. Units 12–20 do not have an **Evaluación**, as each unit is not dependent on the previous one, and only some have **Para estudiar** sections. Unit 21 is a final summing up, and there is some extra vocabulary at the end.

Try to use the book little and often, rather than for long stretches at a time. Leave it somewhere handy, so that you can pick it up for just a few minutes and refresh your mind again with what you were looking at the time before. Above all, *talk*. Talk to other Spanish speakers or learners, if at all possible; failing that, talk to yourself, to inanimate objects, to the imaginary characters in this book (warn your family and friends!). If you can find someone else to learn along with you, that is a great bonus.

Do *all* the exercises, and do them more than once, even to the point of committing them to memory. Make maximum use of the cassette: play it as background, even when half your mind is on something else – in the car, in the garden, while doing work in the house, and so on – as well as using it when you are actually studying. The main thing is to create a continuous Spanish 'presence', so that what you are learning is always at the front of your mind, and not overlaid with the thousand and one preoccupations we all have in our daily lives. Advice on effective learning is given every so often in the course.

If at any time you feel you are not making progress, in spite of having been working assiduously in the manner described above, put the whole thing away for a day or two. Sometimes our minds need a rest to sort out and embed what we have been learning; the surprising thing is that when we start again we often seem to have improved in the interval when we were not consciously doing anything.

About the symbols

▤   This indicates that the cassette is recommended for the following section.

◖◗   This indicates a dialogue or monologue.

▥   This indicates a reading passage.

☑   This indicates exercises – places where you can practise using the language.

⚲   This indicates key words or phrases.

⚙   This indicates grammar or explanations – the nuts and bolts of the language.

✳   This draws your attention to points to be noted.

▤   ——————— **Pronunciation guide** ———————

If you have the cassette, listen to it as you work through this introductory section. If you don't, follow the guidelines on how to pronounce certain letters and combinations of letters. Listening to and imitating native speakers is of course the best way to work on your pronunciation.

Spanish has no **w**, but it has three letters in its alphabet that do not exist as such in English.

The first is **ch**, which is pronounced as in English *church*. You will find that the words beginning with **ch** have their own section in the Spanish dictionary, between **c** and **d**.

The second is **ll**, which is pronounced like the *lli* in *million*:

Sevilla, paella, millón. In a Spanish dictionary, words beginning with **ll** have their own separate section immediately after the **l** section – **ll** is a separate letter in Spanish, though it looks like a double **l** in English.

The third 'new' letter is **ñ**, which is different from **n**, and is pronounced like the *ni* in *onion*: señor, señorita, España. There are no common words beginning with **ñ**.

So the whole Spanish alphabet is as follows. If you have the cassette, listen to how it sounds when recited in Spanish.

a b c ch d e f g h i j (k) l ll m n ñ o p q r s t u v x y z.

Spanish vowels

Spanish vowels have very pure sounds, and only one sound each. It is important you try to get these right:

a is nearer to southern English *cup* than *cap*: casa, mañana, Salamanca.

e as in *egg*: Enrique, Benavente.

i as **ee** in *feet*: fino, finísimo, quiquiriquí (cock-a-doodle-doo, pronounced keekeereekee).

o as in *pot* – never as in *know* or *toe*. Pedro, Rodrigo, Santiago de Compostela.

u as in *pool*: Úbeda, Burgos, Lugo. But **u** is silent when it occurs between **g** and **e** or **i**: guerra, guía, Guernica, unless it has two dots over it: Sigüenza, güisqui (*whisky*).

Spanish consonants

Some consonants sound different in Spanish from what we are used to in English:

b and **v** tend to be the same sound – a sort of breathy **bv**: try Barcelona, Valencia, and Vizcaya, Álava, Bilbao.

z is always pronounced **th** as in *thing*: Zamora, Zafra.

c is pronounced the same way when followed by **e** or **i**: Barcelona, Valencia. Now try: civilización.

d is much softer than in English, especially when it is final, where it becomes almost **th**: Madrid, Valladolid, El Cid.

h is never sounded: Huesca, Huelva, Majadahonda, Alhambra.

j is always guttural, rather like the scottish **ch** in loch: Jaén, José, Jijona.

g is guttural like **j** when followed by an **e** or **i**: Jorge, Gijón but 'hard' as in English **g**ut when followed by **a**, **o** or **u**.

qu always sounds **k**, never **kw** – quiosco (*a kiosk*), Jadraque. (The letter **k** only exists in Spanish in a few words of foreign origin such as kilogramo, kilómetro, Kodak.)

r is always trilled – one or two flips of the tongue-tip – and **rr** is even stronger: Granada, Coruña, Rodrigo, Guadarrama, Torrejón.

The stress rules

Spanish words are stressed on the *last syllable* if they end in a consonant other than **n** or **s**: Valladolid, El Escorial, Santander, Gibraltar.

They are stressed on the *syllable before last* if they end in **n** or **s** or a vowel: Granada, Toledo, Valdepeñas.

If a word breaks either of these rules, an accent is written to show where the stress falls: José, Gijón, kilómetro, Cádiz, Málaga, civilización. (All words ending in **-ión** bear this accent.) So if you see a word with a written accent, you must stress the syllable where the accent is placed. The only other use of accents that you need to know is that an accent is placed on *si* to distinguish **sí** (yes) from **si** (if).

Now practise your pronunciation by saying these place names, and check on the map, on the next page, to see where they are.

1	La Coruña	13	Santiago de Compostela
2	San Sebastián	14	Bilbao
3	Burgos	15	Pamplona
4	Zaragoza	16	Barcelona
5	Tarragona	17	Valladolid
6	Salamanca	18	Zamora
7	Madrid	19	Toledo
8	Cuenca	20	Albacete
9	Badajoz	21	Cáceres
10	Sevilla	22	Córdoba
11	Granada	23	Almería
12	Málaga	24	Cádiz

✔ ———— **The bare essentials** ————

Here are some essentials which you need to learn, and can also use for pronunciation practice:

Greetings	**Buenos días**
	Buenas tardes
	Buenas noches
	Hola
Goodbyes	**Adiós**
	Hasta luego

We will talk about how these are used in Unit 1.
Now practise saying these courtesy phrases:

Please	**Por favor**
Thank you	**Gracias; muchas gracias**
Not at all	**De nada**
I'm sorry	**Perdone**

Useful emergency phrases are

May I?	**¿Se puede?**

(if you want to take a chair, open a window, push through a knot of people etc.)

That's enough, thank you.	**Basta, gracias.**

(Use it in a restaurant if your plate is getting too full)

I don't understand.	**No entiendo.**
I don't know.	**No sé**

1

¿QUIÉN ES QUIÉN?
Who's who?

In this unit you will learn

- how to say who you are
- how to ask and say who someone else is
- how to give your name and ask for someone else's
- basic courtesies

Antes de empezar   *Before you start*

Make sure you have read the study guide in the **Introduction**, which gives some helpful advice on how to make the most of this course. If you have the cassette, use it as much and as often as you can, taking advantage of the pause button to practise repeating phrases until you can say them naturally.

◢ ———————— Actividad 1 ————————

It's likely that you already know a few words of Spanish. If you can think of any, such as the words for *hello, thank you, please,* say them aloud and then check the following word list to see whether you were right.

buenos días, señor	good day (sir) (used till about 3pm)
buenas tardes, señorita	good afternoon (miss) (used till late evening)
buenas noches, señora	good night (madam)
hasta luego	see you later
gracias	thank you
por favor	please
sí	yes
no	no
hola	hello
perdone	sorry, excuse me
de nada	that's all right, don't mention it

Comentario

The Spanish greetings **Buenos días, Buenas tardes, Buenas noches** do not correspond exactly to the English *Good morning/Good day, Good afternoon, Good evening/Good night.* **Buenos días** is used during the first part of the day until roughly the time of the main meal which, for most Spaniards, is around 2pm or even as late as 3pm. After that, **Buenas tardes** is used. **Buenas noches** is used only late in the evening or when someone is going to bed. **Hola**, an informal greeting equivalent to hello, can be used at any time.

When saying goodbye, **hasta luego** is the way to say *goodbye for now*, or *see you later*. **Adiós** means *goodbye*, and should be used when you don't expect to see that person again for a while.

———————— Diálogo 1 ————————

Isabel is going to meet some of Paco's colleagues. Before the party, he shows her some pictures (see page 11). She asks Paco to tell her who various people are.

Isabel	¿Quién es este señor?
Paco	Es el señor Ortega.
Isabel	Esta señora, ¿es Luisa?
Paco	No. No es Luisa, es Juanita.
Isabel	Y estos señores, ¿quiénes son?
Paco	Estos son los señores Herrero.

(Later Isabel introduces herself to one of them.)

Isabel	Señor Herrero, buenas tardes.
Sr. Ortega	No soy el señor Herrero, soy el señor Ortega.
Isabel	Oh, perdone, señor…
Sr. Ortega	De nada, señorita. Y ¿quién es Vd? Vd. es Isabel, ¿no?
Isabel	Sí, soy Isabel.

este señor	this man/gentleman
esta señora/señorita	this woman/lady
esta señorita	this girl
estos señores	these people/ladies and gentlemen
es	he/she/it is, you are
son	they are, you are (plural)
¿quién es?	who is (he/she/it)/who are you?
¿quiénes son?	who are (they)?
soy	I am
Usted, ustedes	you (usually written **Vd.**, **Vds.**, but pronounced **usted**, **ustedes**)

Para estudiar

1 Masculine and feminine words

In the dialogue you have encountered **este señor** and **esta señora**. **Este** and **esta** are the masculine and feminine forms of the same word, which we have to use because **señor** is masculine and **señora** is feminine. All names of things in Spanish are either masculine or feminine, not only the obvious ones like man and woman, boy and girl. This distinction is known as the gender of the word. You can often tell a word's gender from its ending: for example, almost all words ending in **-o** are masculine, and those ending in **-a** are mostly feminine. Gender is important because it affects the other words in a sentence. There is more on this in the next unit. Don't worry if this is a new idea that seems strange – in practice it causes no great difficulty in Spanish.

2 Estos *These*

Estos is used with plural words referring to several masculine things/people or to a mixed group of things/people, e.g. **estos señores,** meaning *these men* or *these men and women*.

3 Questions

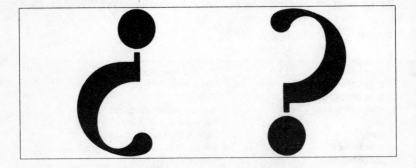

In Spanish, it is easy to make a question. One way is to add **¿no?** to the end of the statement, remembering to raise your voice to give a questioning tone at the end of the sentence. This has the same effect as using *isn't it, aren't you,* etc. in English.

Vd. es Isabel.	*You are Isabel.*
Vd. es Isabel, ¿no?	*Are you Isabel?*

Another way is to turn **Vd. es, Vds. son** round:

¿Es Vd. Isabel?	*Are you Isabel?*
¿Son Vds. los señores Herrero?	*Are you Mr and Mrs Herrero?*

You will have noticed that in written Spanish two question marks are used to identify a question – an inverted one at the beginning as well as the standard one at the end. If only part of the sentence is really the question, the question marks go round that part, as in **Vd. es Isabel, ¿no?** Exclamation marks work in the same way: **Paco ¡es Vd.!** *Paco, it's you!.*

4 *Formal* you

Usted (plural **Ustedes**) means *you,* and is used except when talking to people you know very well or to children (or animals or God). In writing it is almost always abbreviated to **Vd.** (plural **Vds.**) There is another, less formal, way of saying *you,* but you won't need this until Unit 11.

5 *How to be negative*

When you want to say that something is *not* the case, simply put **no** before the word that tells you what is happening (the verb). You have in fact already seen this in **No,** *No* **es Luisa** and *No* **soy el señor Herrero.**

——————— Actividades ———————

2 How would you greet the following people at the times shown?

— **13** —

(a) a male business acquaintance, at 10am
(b) a girl you know well, at 1pm
(c) an older couple you have met a few times, at 6pm
(d) a friend at a party at, 9pm
(e) your family when you are going to bed, at 11pm

3 Someone asks you to tell them who the following characters are. Answer using the information given.
(a) ¿Quién es este señor? (*Paco*)
(b) ¿Quién es esta señorita? (*Isabel*)
(c) ¿Quién es esta señora? (*Sra. Ortega*)
(d) ¿Quiénes son estos señores? (*Sres. Herrero*)
(e) Este señor, ¿es Pedro? (*Paco*)
(f) Esta señorita, ¿es Luisa? (*Isabel*)
(g) Estos señores, ¿son los señores García? (*Sres. Alba*)

4 Turn the following statements into questions by adding **¿no?** in (a), (b), (c) or changing the order of the words in (d) and (e).
(a) Estos señores son los señores Méndez.
(b) Este señor es Paco.
(c) Esta señorita es Juanita.
(d) Vd. es Paco.
(e) Vds. son los señores Alba.

¿Cómo se llama?
What's your name?

Diálogo 2

This time Paco is invited as a guest to Isabel's party and he won't know everyone there. He asks her to identify a few people from her photo album.

Paco	¿Cómo se llama esta señorita?
Isabel	Se llama Ana.
Paco	Y este señor, ¿cómo se llama?
Isabel	Este es el señor Carrera.

Paco	Estos señores, ¿quiénes son?
Isabel	Son los señores Alba.

At the party Paco introduces himself to Mr and Mrs Alba – he has a better memory than Isabel!

Paco	Buenas tardes, señores. Me llamo Paco. Vds. son los señores Alba, ¿no?
Sra. Alba	Sí, somos los señores Alba.

se llama	he/she is called, you are called
me llamo	I am called, my name is
¿Cómo se llama Vd.?	What (lit. *how*) are you called, what is your name?
somos	we are

Para estudiar

1 Me llamo   *My name is*

Another way of identifying yourself and other people is to use **me llamo** *I am called* or *my name is*, and **se llama** *he/she is called, you are called*. To ask someone's name, use the word **¿Cómo?** at the beginning of the question:

¿Cómo se llama?	*What is his/her/its name?; what is he/she/it called?*
¿Cómo se llama Vd?	*What is your name?; what are you called?*

2 More on questions

You will have seen that question words or 'interrogatives', as they are known, such as **¿quién?** *who?* and **¿cómo?** *how?* have an accent. This is not to indicate where the stress falls (see Pronunciation Guide p. 4) but to show that the word is being used in a question, not in a statement. You will find them used without accents, in statements.

Documento número 1

HOTEL **

SAN NICOLAS

Plaza de Armas, 6 – Teléfono (943) 64 42 78
20.280 HONDARRIBIA

¿Cómo se llama este hotel?

 ——————— **Actividades** ———————

5 Give the questions to which these would be answers.
   (a) Me llamo Paco.
   (b) Se llama Isabel.
   (c) Me llamo señora Méndez.
   (d) Se llama señor Méndez.
   (e) No. No me llamo Pedro. Me llamo Paco.
   (f) No. No se llama Luisa. Se llama Isabel.
   (g) Sí. Somos Pedro y Conchita Ortega.

6 Fill in the grid, using the clues given, and column **A** will reveal
   a word you will use on your departure from Spain.
   (a) a way of introducing yourself
   (b) what you would say if you bumped into someone
   (c) you're trying to find out who someone is
   (d) a greeting used between friends
   (e) you have to go but you'll be back soon – what would you
   say?

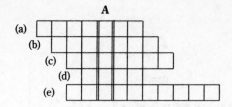

Congratulations! You have completed the first unit of the course. There was a lot to learn in this unit, and it's important to make sure you've understood it all properly before proceeding to Unit 2. Remember to use the answers (**Clave**) at the back of the book to check how well you've done in the **Actividades**, and keep listening to/repeating phrases until they are thoroughly familiar. Then make a final check of your memory and understanding of the material in Unit 1 by trying the little test below.

Evaluación

How would you do the following?
1 Ask someone who they are (two ways).
2 Tell someone who you are (two ways).
3 Check with someone 'Is your name...?'
4 Apologise because you've knocked over a girl's drink.
5 Identify a couple as Mr and Mrs Méndez.

2

¿DE DÓNDE ES?

Where are you from?

In this unit you will learn

- how to ask where people are from
- how to find out someone's nationality and tell them yours

 —————— **Diálogo** ——————

Listen to (or read) the dialogue twice, pausing to repeat the phrases.

Sra. Méndez	¿De dónde es, Paco?
Paco	Soy de Madrid. Soy madrileño. Y ¿Vd.?
Sra. Méndez	Soy de Madrid también. Soy madrileña.
Paco	Y Ana, es española, ¿verdad?
Sra. Méndez	Sí, es española, es catalana. Los señores Alba son españoles también.
Paco	¿De dónde son?
Sra. Méndez	Son de Sevilla los dos.

¿de dónde es...¿de dónde son...?	where is ... from? where are ... from?
también	also
madrileño	from Madrid/a man/person from Madrid
madrileña	from Madrid/a woman from Madrid
los dos	the two, both

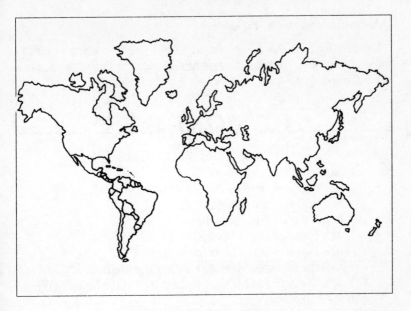

Para estudiar

Nationality

To say your nationality or someone else's, use the words **soy, es, somos, son** as you did to identify people, and add the nationality description: **soy inglés, es español/española**. Note that the ending of the nationality word must change according to the gender of the person described. It also changes if you are talking about more than one person: **somos americanos, son franceses**. Here are a few examples with the masculine, feminine and plural forms:

country	*masculine*	*feminine*	*plural*
América	americano	americana	americanos
Australia	australiano	australiana	australianos
Italia	italiano	italiana	italianos
Francia	francés	francesa	franceses
Escocia	escocés	escocesa	escoceses
Irlanda	irlandés	irlandesa	irlandeses
Alemania	alemán	alemana	alemanes

Alemania is *Germany* in Spanish.

These nationality words are also the ones you use when you want to say *a Spanish woman, a Frenchman,* etc. **Un francés** means *a Frenchman*.

☑ ——————————— **Actividad** ———————————

1   (a) Say where you are from.
    (b) Say that you are English (or whatever)
    (c) Say that you are not Spanish.
    (d) Ask Paco if he is Spanish.
    (e) Ask Isabel if she is Spanish.
    (f) Ask Isabel where she is from.
    (g) Ask the señores Méndez where they are from.
    (h) Ask the señores Méndez if they are from Madrid. (What will they answer?)
    (i) Ask the señores Méndez if they are Spanish. (What will they answer?)
    (j) Say that you and your companion are English.
    (k) Say that you and your companion are not Spanish.

📷 **Comentario**

Not all Spaniards will say **soy español(a).** Some for example, may insist, **Soy catalán, Soy catalana, Soy de Cataluña, Somos catalanes, Somos de Cataluña,** if they are from the north-east of Spain or Barcelona.

People from the Basque country are likely to think of themselves as Basques rather than Spaniards and will say: **Soy vasco, Soy vasca, Soy de Euzkadi, Somos vascos, Somos de Euzkadi.** **Euzkadi** is the Basque word for the Basque region.

It is important to be aware of the strong regional, or some would say national, sensibilities within Spain, particularly in those regions which still use their own separate languages, such as Cataluña and the Basque country.

The Basque language is quite different from Spanish. It is a very ancient language and exceptionally difficult to learn. Catalán, too, is a separate language from Spanish, and has to be learned separately, but unlike Basque it is closely related to Spanish as it also derives from Latin. Sometimes the Spanish language is referred to as **castellano** or 'Castilian'. A man from Barcelona (the capital of Cataluña) could say: **Soy de Barcelona. Soy barcelonés. Soy catalán y también español. Hablo** *(I speak)* **catalán y también castellano.**

All Spaniards are very attached to their home region, even if they have moved away from it. It is in recognition of this regional loyalty that Spain is divided into **autonomías** or regions with a good deal of local self-government. Local pride is also evident in people's attachment and loyalty to their home town or city. Unlike in English, where we only have a few words like 'Londoner' or 'Mancunian', Spanish has a word for the inhabitants of all towns of any size. For example, a man from Seville would describe himself as **un sevillano**.

———————— Actividad ————————

2   Say where the following are from eg.**Un sevillano es de Sevilla** – a **sevillano** is from Seville. Note *un* **sevillano**, *a* man from Seville. Not all of them are obvious, so look back at the map in the introduction, on page 7.

    (a)   Un sevillano.   Un madrileño.   Un barcelonés.

    (b)   Un granadino.   Un cordobés.   Un malagueño.

    (c)   Un burgalés.   Un zaragozano.   Un tarraconense.

    (d)   Un toledano.   Un salmantino.   Un vallisoletano (!)

    (e)   Un zamorano.   Un conquense.   Un gaditano (!!)

    (f)   Un donostiarra (!!!)

———————— Para estudiar ————————

1   Un, una   *A, an*

As you saw in the phrase given above for *a Frenchman* the word for *a* in Spanish is **un**. It changes to **una** when used with a feminine word. Note also that in the sort of sentence shown in the first three examples below, the descriptive word *follows* the word for the person in Spanish:

Un señor español	*A Spanish man*
Una señorita francesa	*A French girl*
Una señora vasca	*A Basque lady*
Un irlandés	*An Irishman*
Una inglesa	*An English woman*

Look again at the list in **Actividad 2**. There you have a list of male/masculine inhabitants of a number of Spanish cities: a Sevillian, a Cordoban, etc. If we wished to indicate a female inhabitant, **un** would become **una**, and all words ending in -**o** would change to -**a**, thus:

Una sevillana. Una madrileña. Una granadina. Una gaditana. Those ending in -**s** would add an -**a**:

Una barcelonesa. Una cordobesa. Una burgalesa. Those ending in -**e** or -**a** already would not change:

Una tarraconense. Una conquense. Una donostiarra. So the word for *a* has two forms, **un** and **una**; in general, (and there are exceptions) you use **un** with a word ending in -**o**, (masculine), and **una** with a word ending in -**a**, (feminine). Words ending with other letters have to be learnt as you go. This masculine/feminine divide applies to everything in Spanish, not just people, as you will see.

2 Languages

The masculine singular form of the nationality description, e.g. **español**, is also the name of the language. So to say that you can speak English and Spanish you say: **Hablo inglés y español.** To say that someone else speaks Spanish you would say: **Habla español.** When you have introduced yourself to a Spanish person or asked their name, using what you have learned in Unit 1, they may well encourage you by saying **Habla español muy bien** *You speak Spanish very well,* even if they do not ask you ¿**Es Vd. español?** or ¿**Es Vd. española?** Notice that in Spanish there is no capital letter on the word for your nationality or the name of the language, only on the name of the country itself – **español, española, españoles, España.**

Actividades

3 The names of seven languages are hidden in this wordsearch. Five are ones that you have encountered in this unit, but there are two that you should be able to guess. The words run across, down, up, backwards and diagonally.

I	G	O	E	R	M	C	P
T	O	S	S	L	A	R	A
A	L	U	P	T	W	S	N
L	F	R	A	N	C	E	S
I	P	L	N	O	R	L	E
A	A	R	O	T	P	G	N
N	Z	M	L	I	F	N	A
O	P	S	E	B	L	I	D

4 You are having a conversation with a Spanish friend, Antonio, about which languages you speak and understand (**entiendo** = *I understand*). Fill in the blanks to complete the dialogue.

Antonio   Vd. habla inglés, ¿verdad?
(a) *You*   *Say yes, you speak English.*
Antonio   ¿Es Vd. americano?
(b) *You*   *Tell him your nationality, and say: you're Catalan, aren't you?*
Antonio   Sí, soy barcelonés. Hablo catalán. ¿Entiende Vd. catalán?
(c) *You*   *Say no, you don't understand Catalán. You speak French and Spanish.*
Antonio   Vd. habla español muy bien.
(d) *You*   *Say thank you very much.*

5 Various people are stating their cities of origin and their native language. Match the cities on the left with the languages on the right.

(a) Soy de Berlín   (i)   hablo inglés
(b) Soy de Londres   (ii)   hablo francés

(c) Soy de Buenos Aires   (iii) hablo catalán
(d) Soy de Barcelona   (iv) hablo alemán
(e) Soy de París   (v) hablo español

Documento número 2

Un pequeño anuncio para Radio 3. El eslogan es 'Somos como somos'. (*A little advertisement for Radio 3. The slogan is 'We are as we are'.* How would you say *I am as I am?*

☑ **Evaluación**

Can you
1 Say where you are from (which town)?
2 Say what nationality you are?
3 Say what language(s) you speak?
4 Tell someone he/she speaks English very well?
5 Ask some one where he/she is from?
6 Ask someone if he/she is Spanish/English etc?
7 Give the masculine and feminine forms to describe people from the following places:
   (a) España (b) Escocia (c) Cataluña (d) Euskadi
   (e) Alemania.

3

MÁS SOBRE VD. MISMO
More about yourself

In this unit you will learn

- how to say where you live and work
- how to ask others what they do and where they do it
- how to give your address
- numbers 0–20

———— Lectura ————

Listen to or read, the following passage about Paco and Isabel.
Key words are given in the list on page 26, but you should be able
to guess the meaning of the words for Paco's and Isabel's jobs.

Paco vive y trabaja en Madrid.
Isabel vive y trabaja en Madrid
también. Paco trabaja como
arquitecto en una oficina de la
calle Goya. Isabel trabaja como
administradora en la oficina
de IBERIA – Líneas Aéreas
de España – en la calle María
de Molina.

Paco trabaja en la calle Goya, pero vive en la calle Meléndez Valdés, en un apartamento. Isabel vive con la familia en un piso de la calle Almagro. El apartamento de Paco es pequeño, pero el piso de la familia de Isabel es muy grande.

vive y trabaja	lives and works	**un piso**	a flat
en	in	**un apartamento**	a small flat
como	as	**pequeño**	small
una oficina	an office	**pero**	but
la calle	the street	**muy**	very
con	with	**grande**	big, large
la familia	the family		

Actividades

1 Respond to the following statements, choosing **verdad** *true* or **falso** *false*.

	Verdad	*Falso*
(a) Isabel vive en Madrid.	☐	☐
(b) Paco vive con la familia de Isabel.	☐	☐
(c) Isabel trabaja en un colegio.	☐	☐
(d) Paco trabaja como profesor.	☐	☐
(e) La oficina de Paco está en Goya.	☐	☐
(f) Paco vive en la calle Meléndez Valdés.	☐	☐

2 Answer the questions.
   (a) ¿Dónde trabaja Paco?
   (b) ¿Dónde vive Paco?
   (c) ¿Dónde trabaja Isabel?
   (d) ¿Dónde vive Isabel?
   (e) ¿Vive Paco en un piso grande?
   (f) ¿Vive Isabel en la calle Goya?
   (g) ¿Quién vive en la calle Meléndez Valdés?
   (h) ¿Quién trabaja en María de Molina?
   (i) ¿Trabaja Paco como administrador?
   (j) ¿De quién es la oficina en María de Molina?

Para estudiar

El, la, los, las *The*

In Unit 2 you found that there are two Spanish words for *a* or *an*: **un** and **una**, used according to the gender of the word to which they are attached. Spanish also has more than one word for *the*: **el** is used with masculine words, and **la** with feminine words. So we have:

> **el apartamento, el piso, el arquitecto, el señor, la oficina, la familia, la señora, la calle** (not all feminine words end in -**a**!)

When *the* precedes a plural word, two new forms are needed. **El** becomes **los** and **la** becomes **las**. So we have:

> **los apartamentos, los pisos, los arquitectos, los señores, las oficinas, las familias, las señoras, las calles**

As you may remember from Unit 1, when you are talking about a person by their name and title, you need to use the definite article (**el, la, los** or **las**), e.g.

El señor Méndez no entiende alemán.	*Mr Méndez doesn't understand German.*
La señorita Carrera es madrileña.	*Miss Carrera is from Madrid.*
Los señores Alba son sevillanos.	*Mr and Mrs Alba are from Seville.*

However, when talking to a person face to face, the definite article is not needed, unless you are asking them who they are.

> Señor Méndez, ¿habla Vd. inglés?
> Buenos días, señorita Carrera.
> ¿Son Vds. **los** señores Alba?

Actividad

3   Fill in the blanks with **el, la, los,** or **las**.
   (a) … apartamentos son generalmente pequeños.

(b) ¿Dónde trabaja … arquitecto?
(c) Isabel vive con … familia.
(d) ¿Dónde están … oficinas de Isabel y Paco?
(e) … señores Méndez son españoles.
(f) Paco vive en … calle Meléndez Valdés.
(g) … piso donde vive Isabel es muy grande.

Para estudiar

¿Qué hace Vd.? *What do you do?*

There are two easy ways of asking what work someone does. One way is to ask **¿Qué hace Vd.?** *What do you do?* Many of the replies may sound similar to English, but in Spanish most of them have a masculine and a feminine form. Here are a few examples of what a person might say when you ask them **¿Qué hace Vd.?**

masculine	feminine	
soy actor	actriz	*actor/actress*
soy profesor	profesora	*teacher*
soy administrador	administradora	*administrator*
soy camarero	camarera	*waiter/waitress*
soy director de empresa	directora de empresa	*company director*
soy enfermero	enfermera	*nurse*

Some words for occupations are the same whether they refer to a man or a woman. These include those ending in **-ista** or **-e**, such as:

un/una taxista	*taxi driver*
un/una artista	*an artist*
un/una periodista	*a journalist*
un/una contable	*an accountant*
un/una interprete	*an interpreter*
un/una estudiante	*a student*

The other way to ask about a person's job is to say **¿Dónde trabaja Vd.?** *Where do you work?* Here are various possible answers to this question:

Trabajo en una oficina.	*I work in an office.*
Trabajo en una agencia de turismo.	*I work in a tourist office/ agency.*
Trabajo en un colegio.	*I work in a school.*
Trabajo en un hospital.	*I work in a hospital.*
Trabajo en casa.	*I work at home.*

Note that **¿Dónde?** and **¿Qué?** are two more examples of words that need accents when they are used to ask a question.

Actividad

4 Match each of the following professions (on the left) with one of the places of work on the right. Some places will be used for more than one answer.

(a) Es profesor – trabaja en…

(b) Soy administradora – trabajo en…

(c) Soy enfermera – trabajo en…

(d) Es arquitecto – trabaja en…

(e) Es actriz – trabaja en…

(f) Soy camarero – trabajo en…

un café

un hospital

un colegio

una oficina

un teatro

Diálogo

Paco and Isabel are being asked by Ricardo where they live and work. Listen to (or read) the dialogue twice before studying the rest of the unit to see how to talk about where you live.

Ricardo	¿Dónde vive Vd., Isabel?
Isabel	Vivo en Madrid, en la calle Almagro.
Ricardo	¿Y dónde trabaja?
Isabel	Trabajo en la calle María de Molina.
Ricardo	¿Y Vd., Paco?
Paco	Vivo en Madrid también.
Ricardo	¿Dónde en Madrid?
Paco	En la calle Meléndez Valdés, numero cinco, tercero D.

Ricardo	¿Y trabaja Vd. en Madrid?
Paco	Sí, trabajo en la calle Goya.

Para estudiar

1 I work, I live, I …

Trabajo and **vivo** mean *I work* and *I live*. When you want to say 'I' do something, you will find that the word almost always ends in -**o**, as in several examples you already know: **hablo, me llamo, entiendo**. There are a very small number of exceptions to this rule, one of which is the word for I am – **soy**.

2 Números 0–20 *Numbers 0–20*

0	cero	11	once
1	uno	12	doce
2	dos	13	trece
3	tres	14	catorce
4	cuatro	15	quince
5	cinco	16	dieciséis
6	seis	17	diecisiete
7	siete	18	dieciocho
8	ocho	19	diecinueve
9	nueve	20	veinte
10	diez		

Learn these thoroughly. Practise them not only in order but at random to help you remember them.

3 ¿Dónde vive? *Where do you live?*

Depending on the context, you might need to give only a vague reply such as **vivo en Madrid** or **vivo en Londres**. On some occasions, however, you may need to give your address, and for visiting Spanish friends or places you will certainly need to understand when someone tells you theirs.

Here is a typical address (**la dirección**).

La dirección de Isabel es:

Señorita Isabel Ballester García
Almargro 14, 6.A
28010 Madrid
España

Notice you do not need to use the word **calle**, although other words, such as **avenida**, **plaza**, **paseo**, are usually not omitted. The figure 6° A stands for *sexto A*, ie., the sixth floor, flat A. 28010 is the code for Madrid (28) and the district (010).

Here is Paco's address: (**Paco** is short for **Francisco**)

Señor Don Francisco Ruiz Gallego
Meléndez Valdés 5, 3·D
28015 Madrid
España

Actividad

5 (a) Ask Paco where he lives. (What will he answer?)
   (b) Ask Isabel where she works. (What will she answer?)
   (c) Tell Paco you also live in a small apartment.
   (d) Tell Isabel you also work in an office.
   (e) Tell her you do not speak Spanish very well yet (**todavía**).
   (f) Give your nationality and say what language you speak.

📷 Comentario

You will have noticed two things. The first is that Isabel and Paco have two surnames. All Spaniards do. They take the first of their father's two names and the first of their mother's. In any case, Spanish women keep their own names on marriage, and take their husband's when being spoken of jointly, as in **los señores Méndez.** If you only want to use one surname, which you normally do for informal use, it must be the first. So Francisco Ruiz Gallego is **Paco Ruiz** to his friends. The other thing you may have noted is the use of **don.** You use it in formal situations with the forename (never with the surname alone). For married women use **doña.** The wife of señor Méndez happens to be **Señora Doña Aurora Lozano Bonet.** No mention of señor Méndez at all! However, **Doña** is not usually used with the names of unmarried women. There is more on this in Unit 12.

☑ ———— Actividad ————

6   The written numbers 0–12 are all – except one – hidden in this wordsearch. They are written backwards, up, down and diagonally as well as across. What is the missing number?

```
L   C   U   A   T   R   O   N
O   T   P   O   R   E   C   R
Z   C   L   T   E   C   N   O
I   O   H   V   S   E   I   S
E   N   E   O   C   C   C   A
D   U   D   N   T   O   M   L
N   R   O   E   A   D   I   P
```

☑ Evaluación

Can you do the following?
1   Count backwards from 20 to zero.
2   Say where Paco lives.
3   Ask Isabel what she does and where she works.
4   Say that you are a company director.

— **32** —

5 Say where you live and where you work.

Documento número 3

Some new flats are for sale near the airport.
   (a) How many bedrooms do they have?
   (b) Where can you keep your car?
   (c) What times can you phone the agency?

4
¿CÓMO ESTÁ VD.?
How are you?

In this unit you will learn

- how to ask after others' health and respond to queries about your own
- how to describe people and things
- how to say where things are

Before you start

✔ ──────── Actividad ────────

You can now say a number of things about yourself in Spanish. You should be able to write or say at least six sentences about yourself and where you work and live. Try to come up with a similarly long description of a relative or friend.

──────── Para estudiar ────────

To be or ... to be

You have already learnt the Spanish for *I am, he is* etc:

    soy   I am

es	he/she/it is
Vd. es	you are
somos	we are
son	they are
Vds. son	you are (plural)

However, we use a different set of words for *I am, you are,* etc. if we are saying where we are, or where things are, or if we are saying how we feel, or what state we are in – tired, pleased, ill, well, married or single and so on.

For example, imagine a gossipy man boring his neighbour on the beach with following monologue. He doesn't wait for many answers, but notice how he switches from one group of words to the other according to the context. He says **soy** or **es** when he wants to say *what* he is, or *what* something is, but **estoy, está, estamos, están,** in saying or asking *how* or *where* he is, or people and things are.

——————— Monólogo ———————

"**Soy** argentino, pero en este momento **estoy** en España. **Estoy** de vacaciones, y **estoy** muy contento. Mi familia **está** aquí también. **Estamos** todos muy contentos. Y Vd., ¿**está** Vd. de vacaciones? ¿**Está** la familia también? ¿**Es** Vd. millonario? ¿Qué hace Vd. pues? Ah, un artista. Vd. **es** muy famoso, **estoy** seguro."

estoy de vacaciones	I am on holiday
están	they are/you (plural) are
estoy contento/seguro	I am pleased/sure
estamos contentos	we are pleased
aquí	here
todo/toda/todos/todas	all, every

——————— Para estudiar ———————

Soy o estoy, *I am*

So our Spanish friends would say:

Soy Paco. Estoy soltero (*single*).
Soy Isabel. Estoy soltera.
Somos los señores Méndez. Estamos casados (*married*).

And we can say about them:

Paco es español. Está soltero.
Isabel es española. Está soltera también, pero los señores Méndez están casados, naturalmente (*of course*).
 Perhaps the commonest use of these words is in: **¿Cómo está Vd? ¿Cómo están Vds?** *How are you*?

To which you answer:

Estoy bien, gracias. Estamos bien, gracias. ¿Y Vd? ¿Y Vds? *I'm fine, thank you. We're fine, thank you. And you?*
You can ask after third parties, as in:
¿Cómo está Paco? ¿Cómo están los señores Méndez?
To which you hope to hear the answer:
Está bien. Están muy bien los dos. *He's fine. They are both very well.*

✳ Now here is a subtle point. If you ask **¿Cómo *es* Paco?** You are asking what he is like – tall, short, friendly, etc. If you ask **¿Cómo *está* Paco?** you want to know whether he is well, happy, tired and so on.

We said above **Paco está soltero**. This suggests that he is single at the moment, but will probably marry. If you say **Paco es soltero** you are suggesting that he is a confirmed bachelor. You can knock on Isabel's door and ask **¿Está Isabel?** That is to say *Is Isabel in?* i.e. you are asking about where she is rather than what she is. You will get the answer **Sí está** or **No, no está**.

☑ ———————— **Actividades** ————————

1   Make eight truthful sentences from these three columns:

Paco		una compañía importante
Isabel		madrileños
Los señores Méndez	es	en la calle Goya

El apartamento de Paco	está	madrileña
IBERIA	son	pequeño
Isabel y Paco	están	muy grande
El piso de Isabel		casados
La oficina de Paco		español

2 Choose one of the following to fill the blanks in each sentence: **no es   no está   no son   no están.**

(a) Isabel y Paco . . . . casados.

(b) Isabel . . . . catalana.

(c) El señor Méndez . . . . barcelonés.

(d) La calle Goya . . . . en Sevilla.

(e) En general, los taxistas . . . . millonarios.

(f) Doña Aurora y doña Luisa . . . . contentas.

(g) París . . . . en España.

(h) Los terroristas . . . . simpáticos.

Remember to check your sentences with the **Clave** at the end of the book.

To sum up: we use **soy, es, somos** and **son** to indicate *characteristics* (permanent) and **estoy, está, estamos** and **están** to indicate *states* (temporary) as well as *position* (both temporary and permanent).

Documento número 4

C/ San Segundo, 40 - Telfs. (918) 25 20 56 - 25 52 61 - 05001 ÁVILA

(a) ¿Cómo se llama este restaurante?

(b) ¿Dónde está?
(c) ¿En qué calle está?

(**Horno de asar** indicates that it specialises in roasts; **un horno** is an oven; **asar** is the word for to roast.)

Diálogo

Ricardo meets Paco and enquires about Isabel. Listen to (or read) the dialogue, checking the key words given below, and practising saying each of the phrases aloud.

Ricardo   ¿Cómo está Vd., Paco?
Paco   Estoy muy bien, gracias. ¿Y Vd.?
Ricardo   Muy bien. ¿Dónde está Isabel?
Paco   Está en casa.
Ricardo   ¿En casa? ¿No trabaja? ¿Está de vacaciones?
Paco   No, no está de vacaciones. No está muy bien. Está constipada.
Ricardo   Entonces la llamo por teléfono. ¿Qué número es?
Paco   Es el 2171806 (dos, diecisiete, dieciocho, cero seis).

está constipada	she has a cold
entonces	then
la llamo por teléfono	I'll give her a ring

Comentario

Phone numbers

Phone numbers are usually given in pairs of figures. If there is an odd number of figures, the one at the beginning is treated singly. So 2121611 is said as **dos, doce, dieciséis, once**, while 101420 would be said as **diez, catorce, veinte**.

—————— Actividades ——————

3 A Spanish friend is talking to you about your English colleague whom he met on a visit to England. Complete the dialogue.

Antonio   ¿Cómo está Jane?
(a) *You*   *Say she's very well*
Antonio   ¿Está todavía (*still*) soltera?
(b) *You*   *Say no, she is married to* (con) *Paul.*
Antonio   ¡Qué bien! ¿Están contentos los dos?
(c) *You*   *Say yes, of course.*
Antonio   ¿Y cómo es Paul?
(d) *You*   *Say he is very nice. He is a Scotsman.*
Antonio   ¿Y dónde viven?
(e) *You*   *Say they live in Edinburgh.*
Antonio   ¿Qué hace Paul?
(f) *You*   *Say he's an accountant and works in Edinburgh.*
Antonio   Muy bien, Y Jane, ¿trabaja in Edimburgo también?
(g) *You*   *Say yes, she works in a tourist agency.*

4 Speaking of **Paco**, say that:
(a) he is very well.
(b) he is not very well.
(c) he is an architect.
(d) he is at home.
(e) he is on holiday.
(f) he is pleased.
(g) he is from Madrid.
(h) he is in Madrid.
(i) he is Spanish.
(j) he has a cold.

Check in the key that you have used **es** and **está** correctly, and then repeat the exercise, speaking of **los señores Méndez**:

5 (a) they are very well.
(b) they are not very well.
(c) they are friendly.
(d) they are at home.
(e) they are on holiday.

(f) they are pleased.
(g) they are from Madrid.
(h) they are in Madrid.
(i) they are Spaniards.
(j) they have colds.

Para estudiar

Adjectives

Descriptive words such as **grande, pequeño, soltero**, etc. are known as adjectives, and in Spanish they must 'agree' with the person(s) or thing(s) they describe. This means that, as with the words for occupations that you met in Unit 3, the endings of the adjective must be masculine or feminine, singular or plural, e.g. *Paco* no está casado, *los* apartamentos son pequeños, *Isabel* está contenta, las enfermeras son simpáticas, etc.

Adjectives ending in **-e** are the same for both genders, but take an **-s** in the plural:

Paco es inteligente.
Isabel es inteligente.
Los señores Mendez son muy inteligentes.

When you are not saying *the gentleman is married* but simply *a married gentleman*, the adjective **casado** always comes *after* the noun **un señor**. Here are a few more examples: **un piso grande** *a large flat*, **una chica antipática** *a horrible girl*, **un chico alto** *a tall boy*, **una señora contenta**, *a happy lady*.

Evaluación

Can you do the following?
1 Say you are pleased.
2 Say you are on holiday.
3 Ask someone what their job is.
4 Say you are married/single.

5 Ask if Paco is at home when you arrive at the flat.
6 Ask after someone's health.
7 Say you are well/not very well.

5

NUESTRAS FAMILIAS
Our families

In this unit you will learn

- how to give details, and ask for information, about families and personal circumstances
- how to say what things belong to whom
- how to say *there is* and *there are*

Preámbulo

Two useful verbs: have and say

You have already learned how to use some different parts of verbs according to who is doing the action, for example **habla** *he/she/it speaks, you speak* and **trabajo** *I work*. Here are two important verbs which you need to learn.

tengo	*I have*
tiene	*he/she/it has, you have*
tenemos	*we have*
tienen	*they/you (plural) have*

digo	*I say*
dice	*he/she/it says, you say*
decimos	*we say*
dicen	*they/you (plural) say*

Lectura 1

Listen to (or read) Isabel's description of her family two or three times, pausing after every sentence to practise repeating the Spanish.

La familia de Isabel

Isabel dice:
Somos seis en mi familia: mi padre, mi madre, y cuatro hijos. Tengo una hermana y dos hermanos. Mi hermana se llama Margarita y mis hermanos se llaman Fernando y José Antonio. Margarita está casada. Su marido se llama Luis Méndez. Es el hijo de los señores Méndez. Margarita y Luis tienen un hijo – Luisito.

Fernando y José Antonio no están casados. Viven en casa con mis padres. Afortunadamente tenemos un piso grande. Mi madre tiene también un perro. Es muy pequeño y simpático. Se llama Chispa.

somos seis en la familia	there are six of us in the family
mi padre	my father
mi madre	my mother
hijo	son
hija	daughter
hijos	children
hermano	brother
hermana	sister
hermanos	brothers/brothers and sisters
marido	husband
mujer	wife
un perro	a dog
simpático	nice
afortunadamente	fortunately

Para estudiar

My, your, his, her, its

The words that denote who someone or something belongs to are
very easy to use in Spanish. **Mi** *my* is used with both masculine
and feminine words (**mi padre, mi madre**), and has an **-s** added
when used with plural words (**mis padres**). The words **su** and
sus are particularly useful as they are the equivalent of several
English words. **Su** is used with singular words and means
his/her/it/your/their, depending on the context; **sus** works in exactly the same way with plural words. Like **mi** and **mis, su** and
sus are not affected by gender. For example:

mi nieto	my grandson
mis nietas	my granddaughters
su hermano	his/her/your/their brother
su hermana	his/her/your/their sister
sus abuelos	his/her/your/their grandparents
sus tías	his/her/your/their aunts

Lectura 2

So here is a diagram of Isabel's family..

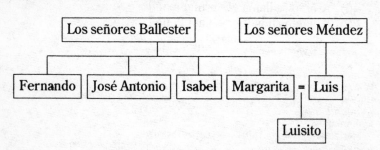

Fernando y José Antonio son los hermanos de Isabel y Margarita.
Isabel y Margarita son las hermanas de Fernando y José Antonio.
Sus padres son los señores Ballester. Los señores Ballester y los
señores Méndez son los abuelos (abuelo/abuela) de Luisito.

Luisito es su nieto. Luisito es el sobrino de Fernando, de José Antonio y de Isabel. Isabel es la tía de Luisito; Fernando y José Antonio son los tíos. Isabel y Luis son cuñados. Los señores Ballester son los suegros de Luis; los señores Méndez son los suegros de Margarita.

sobrino	nephew
sobrina	niece
tía	aunt
tío	uncle
cuñado	brother-in-law
cuñada	sister-in-law
suegros	parents-in-law

Actividades

1 Answer the questions:
   (a) ¿Quién es el padre de Luis?
   (b) ¿Cómo se llama el padre de Luisito?
   (c) ¿Cómo se llama la tía de Luisito?
   (d) ¿Cuántos abuelos tiene Luisito?
   (e) ¿Cuántos sobrinos tiene Isabel?
   (f) ¿Quiénes son los suegros de Margarita?
   (g) ¿Y de Luis?
   (h) ¿Quién es la cuñada de Luis?
   (i) ¿Cómo se llama el hermano de José Antonio?
   (j) ¿Cuántos tíos (tíos y tías) tiene Luisito?

2 Complete the following sentences.

Isabel dice:
   (a) Margarita es mi ....
   (b) Fernando y José Antonio son mis ....
   (c) Luis no es ... hermano, es ... .
   (d) ... padres son los ...... de Luisito.

Luisito dice:
   (e) Tengo ...... abuelos.
   (f) ... madre ... . Margarita.
   (g) ... tío Fernando es ... . de mi madre.

Los señores Ballester dicen:

(h) Tenemos ...... hijos y ... nieto.

(i) Tenemos solamente ... ... casada.

(j) Isabel, Fernando y José Antonio no ...... casados, pero ......muchos amigos.

3 Here is some information about another family. Read it carefully, and then as an exercise fill in the missing names on the diagram which follows. You'll need to use the information about Spanish surnames that you learned at the end of Unit 3. The answers, as always, are in the key.

Carlos López Silva está casado con Carmen Rivera García. Tienen tres hijos y tres nietos. Su hija Carmen no está casada pero sus dos hijos Pedro y Diego sí. La mujer de Pedro se llama Ana Serrano, y tienen una hija que también se llama Carmen. Tres mujeres de esta familia se llaman Carmen: la nieta Carmen López Serrano, su tía Carmen López Rivera, y su abuela Carmen Rivera García. La pequeña Carmen tiene dos primos Diego y José María López Ayala, hijos de Diego López Rivera y su mujer María Ayala.

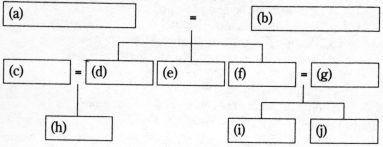

¿Tiene Vd. un coche?
Do you have a car?

Lectura 3

Isabel tells us a few more details about Paco, and Paco talks about Isabel and her family. Listen to what they say (or read the passages if you don't have the cassette).

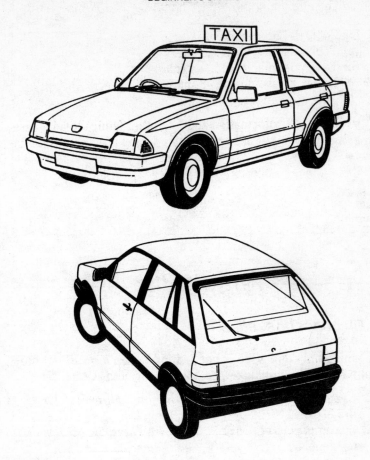

Isabel dice:

Paco vive en la calle Meléndez Valdés. Su apartamento es pequeño pero es suficiente para él. Es un apartamento alquilado. Paco no vive con sus padres, porque ellos viven ahora en Alicante, pero yo vivo con los míos. Paco tiene un coche. Su coche siempre está en la calle porque Paco no tiene garaje.

Paco dice:

Isabel vive en un piso de la calle Almagro, pero el piso no es de ella, naturalmente, es de sus padres, y el coche es de ellos también. Isabel no tiene coche. Dice que no es necesario. Ella y su madre dicen que los taxis son muy convenientes para ellas. Para mí, un coche es más conveniente.

alquilado	rented
ahora	now
porque	because
un coche	a car
siempre	always
él	he, him
ella	she, her
ellos	they, them (m)
ellas	they, them (f)
para él	for him
de ellos	theirs(m)
de ella	hers
para ellas	for them(f)
más	more
para mí	for me

Para estudiar

1 *Él, ella, ellos, ellas*

In Spanish only one word is needed for *he* and *him*. **Él** not only means *he* but also *him*. Likewise, **ella** means both *she* and *her*.

Este apartamento es adequado para **él/ella**.	*This flat is big enough for him/her.*
Él vive aquí, pero **ella** vive en Valencia.	*He lives here, but she lives in Valencia.*

The same dual-purpose rule applies to **ellos** and **ellas** (*they/them*, masculine and feminine).).

2 *Using* no, sí *to make comparisons*

Making a simple comparison between what two people are, do or have, is easier in Spanish than it is in English, as the following examples show:

Isabel vive con la familia, pero Paco **no**.	*Isabel lives with the family, but Paco doesn't.*
Los señores Méndez están casados, pero Isabel y	*Mr and Mrs Méndez are married,but Paco and Isabel*

Paco **no**.

aren't.

La señora no es muy alta,
pero su marido **sí.**

*The lady is not very tall, but
her husband is.*

Mi hermano no está contento,
pero mis padres **sí.**

*My brother is not happy,
but my parents are.*

As we have seen, **vivo** means *I live.* You use the word for *I* – **yo** –
only if you want to stress the *I*: Yo vivo en Madrid, pero Antonio
no. *I live in Madrid but Antonio doesn't.*

Similarly with **él, ella, ellos** and **ellas.** For example:

Yo hablo español, pero él no.
El habla español, pero ella no.

I speak Spanish, but he doesn't.
*He speaks Spanish, but
she doesn't.*

3 *El mío, la mía, los míos, las mías*

These words translate *mine.* You use the one that agrees with the
person or thing that is possessed. For example:

Paco no vive con sus padres, pero
yo vivo con los míos.

*Paco doesn't live with his
but I live with mine.*

¿Cómo se llama su hermana? La
mía se llama Conchita.

*What is your sister's name?
Mine is called Conchita.*

You do not need **él, la, los, las,** though, if you want to say *it's
mine, they're mine.*

¿De quién es este coche? Es mío.
Esta casa es mía.

Whose is this car? It's mine.
This house is mine.

——— Actividad ———

4 Complete these sentences about Paco by adding a contrasting
comment about Isabel. Use the following example as a model:
Paco trabaja como arquitecto, **pero Isabel no.**

(a) Paco vive en un apartamento, …

(b) Paco es alto, …

(c) Paco no vive con la familia, …

(d) Paco no habla alemán, …

(e) Paco no tiene hermanos, …
(f) Paco tiene un coche, …

Para estudiar

4 Hay: *there is, there are.* ¿Hay?: *is there? are there?*

This is an invaluable little word (Be careful not to pronounce the **h**. **Hay** sounds the same as **¡Ay!** which is an exclamation of pain, grief or surprise.) **Hay** has a multiplicity of uses:

¿Cuántas personas hay en la oficina de Paco? Hay siete. Hay tres arquitectos y dos delineantes (*draughtsmen*). También hay un estudiante y una secretaria.

¿Cuántas personas hay en la familia de Isabel? Hay seis: los padres y cuatro hijos. Pero una hija está casada y vive con su marido y su hijo. Hay un perro, que es de la madre de Isabel y que se llama Chispa

¿Cuántos vuelos diarios (*daily flights*) hay de Londres a Madrid? Hay cinco vuelos de Iberia y cuatro de la BA.

Hay is used to indicate availability of goods and services:

En el café:	Hay chocolate con churros.
En el quiosco:	Hay billetes de lotería.
En el restaurante:	Hoy hay fabada.
En el teatro:	No hay entradas.

Churros are a sort of fritter or doughnut which you dunk in hot, thick chocolate. Very fattening but delicious. **Fabada** is a bean stew (see unit 18). The words **billete** and **entrada** are both used for *ticket*, but the former is used for train, bus or lottery tickets (and also banknotes), and the latter for anywhere you pay for entrance, such as the theatre or a museum. **Hoy** means *today*.

Ayuntamiento de Madrid
Area de Cultura, Educación,
Juventud y Deportes

Museo Municipal

362937

ENTRADA GRATUITA

Actividad

5 Answer the questions. As always, the key gives you the fullest answers, but try to convey the essential information even if you can't produce a whole sentence the first time.
   (a) ¿Dónde hay fabada hoy?
   (b) ¿Qué hay en el quiosco?
   (c) ¿Hay entradas para el teatro?
   (d) ¿Cuántos vuelos diarios de la BA hay de Londres a Madrid?
   (e) El apartamento de Paco, ¿es adecuado para él?
   (f) ¿Es de él, o está alquilado?
   (g) ¿Por qué no vive Paco con sus padres?
   (h) ¿Dónde está siempre el coche de Paco?
   (i) El coche de la familia de Isabel, ¿es de ella o de sus padres?
   (j) ¿De quién es el perro en casa de Isabel?

This has been a unit with a lot of new material; read it through again before you try the **Evaluacíon** to see how much you have understood and remembered.

Evaluación

Can you do the following?
1 Say what immediate family you have, and say what their names are?
2 Describe your extended family?
3 Describe your house/home and say who lives in it?

There will be no answers in the **Clave,** so check your use of Spanish with the material in this unit.

6

EN MOVIMIENTO

Moving around

In this unit you will learn

- how to talk about going and returning
- how to discuss means of transport
- how to indicate dates
- numbers 21–31

 ——————— **Para estudiar** ———————

1 Números 21–31

You met numbers 1–20 in Unit 3. Here are the numbers 21 to 31.

21	veintiuno	25	veinticinco	29	veintinueve
22	veintidós	26	veintiséis	30	treinta
23	veintitrés	27	veintisiete	31	treinta y uno
24	veinticuatro	28	veintiocho		

The words for 21–29 are contractions of **veinte y uno, veinte y dos**, etc., but it is only 21–29 that contract; all the later numbers, from 31–39, 41–49 etc., are written as three words, as in **treinta y uno**, above.

MAYO

1	2	3	4	5	6	7
8	9	10	11	12	13	14
15	16	17	18	19	20	21
22	23	24	25	26	27	28
29	30	31				

2 Los meses del año *The months of the year*

enero	*January*	julio	*July*
febrero	*February*	agosto	*August*
marzo	*March*	septiembre	*September*
abril	*April*	octubre	*October*
mayo	*May*	noviembre	*November*
junio	*June*	diciembre	*December*

Note that the names of the months are written *without* a capital letter.

3 La fecha *The date*

Now you know numbers up to 31 and the names of the months of the year, you can give dates.

Written dates are in figures, of course; spoken dates are exactly the same as in English e.g. "the second of May". For example:

el dos de mayo
el veinticinco de diciembre
el diecisiete de septiembre

and so on. If it is already clear which month you are talking about, and you just want to say *the 5th, the 20th,* etc., say **el día** (*the day*) **5, el día 20**, and so on.

✳ **El día** *the day* is another of the few words in Spanish that end in **-a** but are masculine.

✅ ———————————— **Actividades** ————————————

1 Give the Spanish for:
    (a) 1st March   (g) 22nd February
    (b) 16th June   (h) 10th April
    (c) 31st August   (i) 26th October
    (d) 2nd November   (j) 24th December
    (e) 4th July   (k) 30th January
    (f) 19th May   (l) 11th November
2 Practise giving personal and family dates:
    ¿Cuándo es su cumpleaños? (*When is your birthday?*)
    ¿Y él de su padre?/¿madre?/¿marido?/¿mujer?/¿hijo?/¿hija?/
    ¿hermano?/¿hermana?, etc.

▣ ———————————— **Diálogo** ————————————

Ricardo asks Paco about his plans for June. Listen to (or read) the dialogue twice, and try to identify how Paco says *I'm going* and *I'm returning*.

Ricardo	¿Qué hace en junio, Paco?
Paco	En junio voy de viaje.
Ricardo	¿En qué día va Vd.?
Paco	Voy el día 5. Tengo un congreso en Santander el día 6 de junio.
Ricardo	¿Y vuelve a Madrid después del congreso?
Paco	No, tengo una reunión en Barcelona el día 9. Voy directamente de Santander a Barcelona.
Ricardo	¿Cómo va – en tren?
Paco	No, voy en coche. Vuelvo a Madrid el 10 de junio.

voy	I go, I am going
de viaje	on a trip
va	he/she/it goes, you go
vuelvo	I return
vuelve	he/she/it returns, you return
un congreso	a conference
una reunión	a meeting
en tren	by train
en coche	by car
después del congreso	after the conference

——————— Para estudiar ———————

In the above dialogue and vocabulary list, notice the important words **voy** *I go*, and **va** *he/she goes, you go*. Later in this unit we shall have **vamos** *we go*, and **van** *they go*, or *you* (**Vds.**) *go*. However, if you look up *to go* in a dictionary you will find **ir**, which is very different from **voy**, etc.. This is because *to go* in Spanish is a very odd verb, perhaps because it is so constantly used. **Ir** is the name of the verb, the dictionary entry, or, to give it its grammatical name, the infinitive. Usually infinitives are more easily recognisable, and end in **-ar** (most of them), **-er** or **-ir**. For example *to speak* is **hablar**, *to do* is **hacer** and *to live* is **vivir**.

By the way, if someone calls your name, where in English you might reply *Coming!*, in Spanish you call **¡Voy!**. In English where you would say *I'll come with you*, the Spanish would say **Voy con Vd.**, *I'll go with you*.

——————— Actividad ———————

3   Answer the following questions as though you were speaking for Paco:
   (a) ¿Dónde va Vd. en junio, Paco?
   (b) ¿Por qué va a Santander?
   (c) ¿Tiene un congreso también en Barcelona?

(d) ¿Cuándo va a Santander?
(e) ¿Y a Barcelona?
(f) ¿Cómo va?
(g) ¿Qué día vuelve Vd. a Madrid?
(h) ¿Por qué no vuelve a Madrid el 7 de junio?

_____ Los señores Méndez _____ están de vacaciones

_____ Lectura _____

Señora Mendez describes their holiday in Málaga. Listen to (or read) her description noticing how she says *we* do things.

Hoy, 6 de septiembre, estamos de vacaciones. Estamos en Málaga y no volvemos a Madrid hasta el día 30. Pasamos un mes en Málaga. Tenemos un apartamento alquilado. Vamos todos los días al café para tomar el aperitivo. Se puede comer también, pero generalmente volvemos a casa para comer. Después de la siesta visitamos a amigos o vamos al cine o al teatro.

hasta	until
pasar	to spend, pass
todos los días	every day
tomar	to take/have (of refreshment)
comer	to eat/have lunch
se puede	one can

_____ Para estudiar _____

1 Al *and* del

Notice the contraction of **a el** to **al** to give **al cine**, *to the cinema* and **al** teatro, *to the theatre*. **De el** contracts similarly to form **del**, as in los meses **del** año, and as you will now recognise, in Costa **del** Sol (lit. *coast of the sun* – **el sol**).

2 Vamos *We go*

In the passage above, Señora Méndez uses the form: **vamos** *we go.* You will find that almost all words meaning *we* do something end in -**amos, -emos** or -**imos**. There were several examples in señora Méndez's account, some of which you've already come across and some of which are new:

estamos	*we are*
tenemos	*we have*
vamos	*we go*
pasamos	*we spend/we pass*
volvemos	*we return*

Other verbs you already know work similarly. For example, Paco might say:

Isabel y yo **trabajamos** en Madrid los dos. **Vivimos** en Madrid también. **Somos** madrileños. **Hablamos** español.

Spanish verbs fall into three groups, which is why there are three different endings – you will learn more about this in Unit 8. (**Somos** is an odd one out.)

3 Para ... *In order to ...*

In the passage about the Méndez on holiday you came across the phrases **para tomar, para comer**. **Para** means *for*, as you have seen, but also *in order to*. So **para tomar el aperitivo** means *in order to have an aperitif*, or simply *to have an aperitif*.

4 Se puede ... *One can ...*

In señora Mendez's description of their holiday she says **se puede comer en el café** *one can eat at the café*. **Se** can translate *one* when you are talking of people in general. For example, in a shop window you might see **se habla inglés** *English spoken* (lit. *one speaks English*). In Barcelona you could say **aquí se habla catalán** *people speak Catalan here*. You can also use it to ask the way e.g. **¿Cómo se va a la estación de autobuses?** *How does one get to the bus station?* There is more on this very useful construction in Unit 10.

Documento número 5

Cumplimente el cupón adjunto y envíelo a TRIBUNA DE EDICIONES DE MEDIOS INFORMATIVOS, S. A. C/ Orense, 70, 4.ª planta. 28020 Madrid. Aptdo. de Correos 14.763. Tel (91) 571 09 42.

☐ Sírvanse suscribirme a "TRIBUNA de Actualidad" por 1 año (52 números) al precio total de: España: 12.300 ptas. Portugal: 14.500 ptas. Europa y Norte de África: 19.500 ptas. América, Asia y África: 30.100 ptas. Oceanía: 39.000 ptas. (gastos de envío incluidos).

Nombre: ....

Dirección: .... C.P.: ....

Población: .... Provincia: .... Teléfono: ....

Firma:

FORMA DE PAGO QUE DESEO   ☐ Cheque n.º .... que adjunto
☐ Giro postal n.º .... de fecha....................

If you want to subscribe to the magazine *Tribuna* you can complete a coupon like the one on page 58.

(a) How much would it cost to have it sent to the U.K.?
(b) How many issues would you get?
(c) Could you complete the details required?

C.P. stands for the post code **código postal**.

——————— Actividades ———————

4 Answer the following questions as though you were speaking for the señores Méndez.

(a) ¿Por qué están Vds. en Málaga, señores?
(b) ¿Cuándo vuelven Vds. a Madrid?
(c) ¿Cuánto tiempo pasan Vds. en Málaga?
(d) ¿Están Vds. en un hotel?
(e) ¿Dónde van hoy para tomar el aperitivo?
(f) ¿Van mañana también?
(g) ¿Y pasado mañana?
(h) ¿También comen Vds. en el café?
(i) ¿Tienen Vds. familia o amigos en Málaga?
(j) ¿Qué hacen Vds. después de la siesta si no visitan a amigos?

5 Ricardo asks you about your holiday plans for the summer. Complete the dialogue, following the guidelines for your replies.

Ricardo	¿Va Vd. de vacaciones este año?
(a) *You*	*Say yes, you're going to Santander and Madrid.*
Ricardo	¡Qué bien!, ¡va a España! ¿Y cuándo va?
(b) *You*	*Say you're going on 20 July.*
Ricardo	¿Y cuántos días pasa Vd. en Santander?
(c) *You*	*Say you're spending ten days in Santander and then* (después) *you go to Madrid.*
Ricardo	Entonces, va a Madrid el día 31.
(d) *You*	*Say yes, and you're spending five days in Madrid with your friends.*
Ricardo	¿Toma Vd. el avión para ir de Santander a Madrid?
(e) *You*	*Say no, you're taking the train.*
Ricardo	Bien, ¡buenas vacaciones!

Lectura

Viajar en España *Travelling in Spain*

De Madrid se puede tomar el tren o el autobús a todas partes de España. También se puede ir en avión a Barcelona, a Valencia, a Santiago de Compostela, a Bilbao etc.. El avión es más rápido pero es más caro. Es el servico nacional de IBERIA que va a muchas capitales de provincia. El servicio internacional va a Sudamérica, a la América Central y a muchas capitales de Europa. También en junio, julio y agosto hay muchos vuelos charter para los turistas que van a Málaga, a Valencia, a Gerona y a Alicante. El turismo es una industria importante para España.

el avión	the plane	**la capital de**	provincial
se puede tomar	one can take	**provincia**	capital
se puede ir	one can go	**la parte**	part
el/vuelo	flight	**caro**	dear, expensive

Documento número 6

SERVICIO EXPRES

UTILICE EN SUS VIAJES NUESTROS
SERVICIOS ESPECIALES DE LUJO,
VARIAS EXPEDICIONES, DIARIAS
DESDE MADRID A:

VALENCIA
SALAMANCA
BADAJOZ
CACERES
ZAMORA
CUENCA
BENAVENTE

MAS RAPIDOS,
MAS COMODOS Y SEGUROS QUE
CUALQUIER OTRO MEDIO DE TRANS-
PORTE POR CARRETERA QUE VD.
PUEDA ELEGIR.

Auto-Res is a long-distance bus company. They offer a special luxury service to provincial cities, and they say that they are faster, safer and more comfortable than any other means of road transport that you can choose. Find the Spanish for these phrases. **Diario** is a useful word, meaning *daily*.

——————— Actividad ———————

6 Combine one phrase from each column to make eight sensible sentences.

Para visitar les capitales de provincia			el tren, el avión, o el autobús
Para un aperitivo		alquilar	un vuelo charter
Para ir a Barcelona			la siesta
Para ir a Gerona en agosto		ir	a un restaurante
Para pasar un mes en Málaga	se puede	tomar	un vuelo internacional de IBERIA
Para visitar Venezuela		dormir	un piso
Para comer			un coche
Para la digestión después de comer			un gin-tonic

We give the eight most likely versions in the **Clave**.

Evaluación

Check your understanding of Unit 6, before proceeding to Unit 7, by making sure you can do the following:
1 Count backwards from 31 to 21.
2 Recite the months of the year.
3 Give today's date.
4 Ask the way to the theatre.
5 Ask if people speak English here.
6 Say that one can take a bus to the station.
7 Say that there are five flights every day.
8 Say that you spend a month in Spain every year.

7

LLEGADAS Y SALIDAS
Arrivals and departures

In this unit you will learn

- how to talk about arriving and leaving
- how to indicate times
- more about dates
- numbers from 32–199

Preámbulo

Números 32–199

Now you know numbers up to 31, there are not many more words
to learn associated with counting. Here is a complete list of the
'tens':

20	veinte	60	sesenta
30	treinta	70	setenta
40	cuarenta	80	ochenta
50	cincuenta	90	noventa

For the numbers in between, the principle of adding **y** and any other number you need applies all the way through from 30 to 90, e.g.:

33	treinta y tres
58	cincuenta y ocho
71	setenta y uno
99	noventa y nueve

100 is **cien** if it stands by itself, **ciento** if it is followed by another digit. For example:

100	cien
101	ciento uno
110	ciento diez
122	ciento veintidós
137	ciento treinta y siete

Note the difference between the English 137 – *one hundred and thirty-seven*– and the Spanish – **ciento treinta *y* siete**. In Spanish the **y** only occurs between the tens and the units. We won't deal now with the plural hundreds (see Unit 12) but the following will enable you to give current dates in full.

To give the year, string the numbers together starting with **mil**. So the years of the 1990's are:

1991	mil novecientos noventa y uno
1992	mil novecientos noventa *y* dos, etc.

until we reach

1999	mil novecientos noventa y nueve

Then when we reach the year 2000, the date will start with **dos mil** rather than **mil**:

2000	dos mil
2001	dos mil uno
2002	dos mil dos, etc.

Spanish numbers are very straightforward and logical. It is worth making a special effort to learn them really well, as numbers are essential when travelling in a Spanish-speaking country, for shopping, travel times, dates and so on. Practise them until you are fluent by, for example, thinking of the prices in Spanish when you are shopping, working out train times, etc.

—————— **Para estudiar** ——————

1 *Days of the week*

Look at this calendar:

JULIO						
L	M	M	J	V	S	D
	1	2	3	4	5	
6	7	8	9	10	11	12
13	14	15	16	17	18	19
20	21	22	23	24	25	26
27	28	29	30	31		

The week in Spain is always counted from Monday, so the abbreviations along the top for the days of the week – **los días de la semana** – start with that day. Although the abbreviations are in capitals, days of the week, like months, are always written with a small letter:

lunes	Monday
martes	Tuesday
miércoles	Wednesday
jueves	Thursday
viernes	Friday
sábado	Saturday
domingo	Sunday

2 ¿En qué día? ¿En qué fecha? *On what day/date?*

To say that a certain day falls on a certain date, or vice versa, you need a new verb: **caer** *to fall.*

Look at these examples:

    ¿En qué día de la semana   *On what day of the week does*
      cae el dieciséis?   *the sixteenth fall?*

Cae en un jueves.	*It falls on a Thursday.*
¿En qué fechas caen	*On what dates do the*
los domingos en julio?	*Sundays in July fall?*
Caen en el cinco, el doce, el	*They fall on the 5th,*
diecinueve y el veintiséis.	*12th, 19th and 26th.*

Caer also means *to fall* in the usual sense, and goes like this (note the odd 'I' form):

caigo	I fall	**caemos**	we fall
cae	he/she/it falls, you fall	**caen**	they/you (pl.) fall

Actividades

---

1 From the calendar, answer these questions on the same pattern.

(a) ¿En qué día de la semana cae el vientiuno?

(b) ¿En qué día cae el treinta y uno?

(c) ¿En qué fecha cae el primer domingo (*the first Sunday*) del mes?

(d) ¿Y el último domingo? (... *the last Sunday*)

(e) ¿En qué fechas caen los sábados en julio?

(f) ¿En qué día cae el veintisiete?

(g) El quince de julio es el cumpleaños de Isabel – ¿en qué día cae este año?

(h) En julio, ¿el trece cae en martes?

2 Each line of the grid represents one of the days of the week, but they must be entered in a certain order to reveal, in column A, the name of one of the months. Which day goes in which one, and which month is it?

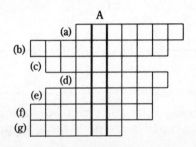

Para estudiar

¿Qué hora es? *What time is it?*

The twenty-four hour clock is used in official timetables, but not in everyday conversation. The usual way of asking and giving the time is shown in the following examples:

¿Qué hora es?	Es la una.	(1.00)
	Es la una y media.	(1.30)
¿Qué hora es?	Son las dos menos cuarto.	(1.45)
	Son las dos.	(2.00)
	Son las dos y cuarto.	(2.15),etc.

Practise saying times in Spanish to yourself in the course of your daily routine, whenever you refer to a clock. To summarise, here is a chart from which you can construct all the times you will need:

Es la una		cinco
Son las dos		diez
Son las tres		cuarto
Son las cuatro	y	veinte
Son las cinco		veinticinco
Son las seis		media
Son las siete		
Son las ocho		veinticinco
Son las nueve	menos	veinte
Son las diez		cuarto
Son las once		diez
Son las doce		cinco

To make things quite clear, you can add **de la mañana** (lit. *of the morning*) for times up till noon, **de la tarde** for the afternoon and early evening, and **de la noche** for 9pm, 10pm, 11pm, and 12pm. For example:

Son las seis de la mañana.
Son las seis y media de la tarde.
Son las diez de la mañana.
Son las diez de la noche.

Notice the difference between **es la una** and **son las dos.** We also say, of course, **son las tres, son las cuatro,** etc. Do not confuse **cuatro** (*four*) with **cuarto** (*a quarter*). *A quarter to four*, and *a quarter past four* will be **las cuatro menos cuarto, las cuatro y cuarto.** Practise saying these.

——————— Diálogo ———————

Isabel habla con el señor Ortega de su viaje a Edimburgo. (*Isabel talks to señor Ortega about her trip to Edinburgh.*)

Listen to (to read) the dialogue at least twice, taking careful note of how Isabel says when things will happen.

Edimburgo/Madrid service

		Dep	Arr	
DAILY (Except Sun)	1B649	0730	1030	DC9 C/Y

Sr. Ortega	¿Qué día va Vd. a Edimburgo? ¿El martes?
Isabel	No. Martes es el día trece. No se puede ir en avion ¡martes y trece! Voy el miércoles, el día 14.
Sr. Ortega	¿A qué hora sale el vuelo?
Isabel	Es el vuelo IB 649. Sale de Madrid a las doce y media y llega a Edimburgo a las tres de la tarde.
Sr. Ortega	¿Tiene amigos en Edimburgo?
Isabel	Sí. Conozco a un matrimonio, Jane y Paul. Jane es amiga mía y va al aeropuerto. Después vamos las dos a su casa.

Sr. Ortega	Y ¿cuándo vuelve a Madrid?
Isabel	Voy a pasar una semana con ellos, y después paso cuatro días en Londres. Vuelvo a Madrid el veintiséis de junio.
Sr. Ortega	Es una vacación bonita. ¡Buen viaje!

el viaje	journey
el avión	plane
salir (sale)	to leave (it leaves)
llegar (llega)	to arrive (it arrives)
el amigo	friend
conocer (conozco)	to know (I know)
un matrimonio	a married couple
bonito	nice, pretty
buen viaje	'bon voyage', have a good journey

Comentario

Isabel is superstitious – she avoids travelling on Tuesday the 13th, the equivalent of our Friday the 13th. A Spanish proverb says **Trece y martes ni te cases ni te embarques** (*On Tuesday the 13th neither marry nor take ship*).

Here is an important point. Notice Isabel says **conozco a un matrimonio**, *I know a married couple*. **Conozco** (verb **conocer**) is *I know* in the sense of being acquainted with, knowing people, places, books, etc. To say *I know* of facts you use **sé** from the verb **saber**. For example:

No **sé** qué hora es.
I don't know what the time is.
¿**Sabe** Vd. cuántos habitantes tiene Madrid? No estoy seguro, pero **sé** que hay más de tres millones.
Do you know how many inhabitants Madrid has? I'm not sure, but I know there are more than three million.

 ——————— **Actividades** ———————

3 Read the following statements and mark whether they are **verdadero** *true*, this has the same meaning as **verdad**, or **falso** (*false*).

	V	F
(a) Isabel va a Edimburgo el día trece.	☐	☐
(b) Su vuelo sale a las doce y media.	☐	☐
(c) Llega a Edimburgo a las tres.	☐	☐
(d) Isabel no tiene amigos en Edimburgo.	☐	☐
(e) Va a pasar una semana en Edimburgo.	☐	☐
(f) Cuando sale de Edimburgo, va a Londres.	☐	☐
(g) Jane y Paul no están casados.	☐	☐
(h) En Edimburgo, Isabel va a un hotel.	☐	☐
(i) Isabel no es supersticiosa.	☐	☐
(j) Edimburgo es la capital de Escocia.	☐	☐

4   Use the IBERIA timetable reproduced below to answer the following questions in Spanish.

IBERIA'S NEW SUMMER SCHEDULES
HEATHROW/MADRID SERVICE

		Dep	Arr	
DAILY (Except Sun)	IB603	0730	1030	DC9 C/Y
DAILY	IB601	1145	1445	Airbus F/C/Y
DAILY)	IB607	1525	1825	B727 C/Y
DAILY (Except Mon)	IB605	1930	2230	Airbus F/C/Y
Mon only	IB605	2030	2330	Airbus F/C/Y

MADRID/HEATHROW SERVICE

		Dep	Arr	
DAILY	IB600	0920	1030	Airbus F/C/Y
DAILY	IB606	1305	1415	B727 C/Y
DAILY (Except Mon)	IB604	1705	1815	Airbus F/C/Y
Mon only	IB604	1805	1915	Airbus F/C/Y
DAILY (Except Sat)	IB602	1955	2105	DC9 C/Y

(a) ¿Cuándo sale el vuelo IB605 de Heathrow los lunes?
(b) ¿Cuándo sale el vuelo IB605 de Heathrow, los otros días la semana?
(c) ¿Cuándo llega el vuelo IB607 a Madrid?
(d) ¿Cuándo sale el vuelo IB600 de Madrid?

(e) ¿Cuándo llega el vuelo IB602 a Heathrow?
(f) ¿Cuándo llega el vuelo IB606 a Heathrow?

You have now covered a great deal of material that will be indispensable on your trip to Spain and in conversation with Spanish friends or colleagues. You can say when things will happen, describe things and people and say where they are, enquire after people's health and do many other useful 'language tasks' in Spanish.

The following **Evaluación** is longer than usual and is intended to help you check that you have understood and remembered some of the main points that we have covered so far. Look back at the relevant unit if you find you have forgotten something. The questions are all personal to you (hence **preguntas impertinentes**, *impertinent questions*) so we cannot give the answers in the key.

☑ Evaluación: preguntas impertinentes

¿Cómo se llama Vd? ¿Es Vd. inglés (inglesa)? ¿Habla Vd. español? ¿Habla Vd. francés?
¿Está Vd. casado (casada) o soltero (soltera)?
¿Es Vd. comunista, socialista, socialdemócrata, liberal, conservador o fascista?
¿Qué hace Vd? ¿Dónde trabaja Vd?
¿Es Vd. millonario? ¿No tiene Vd. mucho dinero?
¿Dónde vive Vd? ¿Vive Vd. en una casa o un piso?
¿Cómo es, grande o pequeño?
¿Cuántas personas hay en su familia? ¿Quiénes son, y cómo se llaman? ¿Tiene una fotografía de su familia?
¿Tiene Vd. un coche? ¿Es necesario un coche para Vd?
¿No son convenientes los taxis para Vd?
¿Es de Vd. este libro de español? ¿Es interesante este libro? ¿Trabaja Vd. mucho con este libro?
¿Va Vd. mucho a España? ¿Por qué? (¿Por qué no?) ¿Va Vd. a España para trabajar o para pasar las vacaciones? ¿En qué mes va Vd. de vacaciones?
¿Cómo va Vd. de vacaciones – en tren, en coche, en autobús o en avión?
¿Sale Vd. de casa todos los días? ¿A qué hora? ¿A qué hora llega

Vd. a casa?

¿Qué hora es en este momento? ¿Que día es? ¿Qué fecha es?
¿Cuándo es su cumpleaños?

¿Es Vd. supersticioso (supersticiosa)? ¿Está Vd. contento (contenta)? ¿Está Vd. preparado (preparada) a estudiar Unit 8?

If you scored well, congratulations – all you need to do is practise
a bit more on those areas where you found the test difficult by listening to or reading the relevant dialogues, checking the **Para
estudiar** sections and making sure you can produce the phrases
yourself; then proceed to Unit 8.

If you found it difficult, it would be worth returning to the units
that covered the material you found problematic and practising by
redoing a few exercises. Perhaps you should go a little more slowly and make more thorough use of the **Clave** every time you have
completed an exercise to make sure you've really mastered one
set of information before moving on to the next.

Remember that it's important to take every opportunity to talk to
and listen to native Spanish speakers, as this is the best way to improve your own accent, fluency and confidence. Once you have really understood the basics, a few spoken mistakes will not prevent
you from being understood and communicating successfully with
a Spanish speaker. Also make sure that you make the most of this
course by following the study guidelines on how to learn, given in
the introduction, adapting them if you prefer to suit the way in
which you learn most easily.

8

DESEOS Y EXIGENCIAS
Wishes and requests

In this unit you will learn

- how to say what you would like
- how to say what you need
- how to buy tickets

🔅 Preámbulo

In Unit 6, we referred to the form of a verb known as the infinitive
– the dictionary entry or 'name' of the verb, usually the form with
to in English: *to speak*, *to eat*, *to live*, etc.. In Spanish these forms
will be words ending in -**ar** (eg. **hablar**), -**er** (eg. **comer**), or -**ir**
(eg. **vivir**). You will already have realised that Spanish works by
changing the ending of these words to indicate who is doing the
action. Thus for *I* the ending will nearly always be -**o** (eg **hablo**, *I
speak*; **como**, *I eat* and **vivo**, *I live*). The exceptions to this are
given below. For the other persons – *he, she, you, we, they* – the
endings are similar to each other but have a characteristic vowel
as you can see:

	-ar	**-er**	**-ir**
I	hablo	como	vivo
he/she/it/you (Vd.)	habla	come	vive
we	hablamos	comemos	vivimos
they/you (Vds.)	hablan	comen	viven

There are, however, lots of oddities and irregularities, so it's best to learn verb forms as you go along – we will point out important deviations from the pattern as they occur. For example, you already know most of the verbs which do *not* end in -o to indicate *I*. They are **soy**, *I am*; **estoy**, *I am*; **voy**, *I go*; **sé**, *I know* and **doy**, *I give*.

——————— Diálogo 1 ———————

Paco's father, Señor Ruiz is buying a plane ticket for a trip to Madrid to visit his son. Listen to (or read) his conversation with the lady at Iberia, and notice how he says what he needs or wants.

Sr Ruiz	Necesito un billete para Madrid, para el jueves.
Señorita	¿Quiere Vd. un billete de ida y vuelta o de ida solo?
Sr. Ruiz	Quiero uno de ida y vuelta, por favor.
Señorita	¿A qué hora quiere salir?
Sr. Ruiz	Necesito estar en Madrid a las tres de la tarde.
Señorita	Hay un vuelo que sale a las doce y cuarto, y llega a la una de la tarde.
Sr Ruiz	Muy bien. ¿Quiere hacer la reserva, por favor?
Señorita	Pues son dieciséis mil pesetas.
Sr. Ruiz	Quisiera pagar con Visa.
Señorita	No hay problema. ¿Necesita Vd. algo más?
Sr Ruiz	No, gracias.

salir	to leave
hacer	to make, do
un billete de ida y vuelta	a return ticket
un billete de ida solo	single ticket
necesitar	to need
necesito estar en Madrid	I need to be in Madrid
¿Quiere hacer la reserva?	Would you make a reservation?
querer	to wish, want, love
¿necesita Vd. algo más?	do you need anything else?
quisiera pagar	I would like to pay

⚏ ————————— Para estudiar —————————

1 Quiero ... *I want ...*

With **quiero** you can simply use the name of whatever item is it that you want, as in the following examples:

Quiero un café.	*I want a coffee.*
Quiero este libro.	*I want this book.*
Quiero dos entradas.	*I want two tickets.*

However, you might need to say that you want to *do* something or *be* something, as in these examples:

Quiero tomar un aperitivo.	*I want to have an aperitif.*
Quiero hablar español.	*I want to speak Spanish.*
Hoy quiero estar in casa.	*Today I want to be at home.*

The verb that follows **quiero** in each of these sentences is in the 'infinitive' form.

✱ **Quiero** can be used with reference to a person (though you also have to insert the little word **a** before the name), but in this context it means *I love* ... . For example:

Quiero mucho **a** mis padres	*I love my parents very much.*
La señora Méndez **quiere a** su marido.	*Mrs Méndez loves her husband.*

2 Quisiera ... *I'd like*

In English there is a difference in tone between the straightforward *I want* and *I would like*, which is less blunt and demanding. A similar difference exists in Spanish between **quiero** and **quisiera**. For example:

Quiero un café.	*I want a coffee.*
Quisiera un café.	*I would like a coffee.*
Quisiera hablar bien el español.	*I'd like to speak Spanish well.*

However, **quiero** is quite acceptable in most circumstances, for example when ordering in a restaurant (as you will see in Unit 18).

Note that **quisiera** ends in **-a** whether it is used with *I* or *he/she/it/you*.

3 Necesito ... *I need* ...

Necesito works in the same way as **quiero** in that it can be used with a noun (the name of something or someone) or with the infinitive form of a verb.

Necesito un billete de ida y vuelta.	*I need a return ticket.*
¿Necesita Vd. viajar a Zaragoza?	*Do you need to travel to Zaragoza?*
Necesitan un coche.	*They need a car.*

Actividades

1 Here are some things that Isabel needs to do in a busy day. Answer the questions for Isabel, saying you would like (**quisiera**) or you need (**necesito**) whatever it is at the time indicated in brackets. The first one is done for you.

(a) ¿Cuándo necesita llegar a la oficina? (0900) (*Necesito llegar a las nueve.*)

(b) ¿A qué hora necesita Vd. salir? (0830)

(c) ¿A qué hora quiere Vd. llamar por teléfono? (1015)

(d) ¿Cuándo necesita hablar con el director? (1145)

(e) ¿A qué hora quiere Vd. comer? (1400)

(f) ¿Cuándo quiere tomar un gin-tonic? (1330)

(g) ¿A qué hora necesita Vd. estar en casa? (1700)

(h) ¿Cuándo necesita ir al dentista? (1730)

(i) ¿Para qué hora quiere Vd. las entradas? (1930)

(j) ¿Para qué hora quiere hacer la reserva en el restaurante? (2230)

(k) ¿A qué hora necesita Vd. salir con el perro? (2400)

2 Listen to (or read) the dialogue again and respond with **Verdadero** or **Falso** to each of the statements.

	V	F
(a) El señor Ruiz quiere tomar el tren.	☐	☐

(b) Quiere un billete de ida solo. □ □
(c) El vuelo sale a las once horas. □ □
(d) Quiere ir a Madrid el jueves. □ □
(e) El señor Ruiz no quiere una reserva. □ □
(f) El señor Ruiz dice que quiere pagar con su □ □
tarjeta de crédito (*credit card*).
(g) El avión llega a Madrid en tres cuartos de hora. □ □
(h) El señor Ruiz paga diez mil pesetas. □ □

☑ **Documento número 7**

Look at the Spanish on this IBERIA boarding pass and compare it
with the English version. Try these questions:
   (a) ¿Para qué fecha es el vuelo?
   (b) ¿Qué número tiene el asiento?
   (c) ¿Es de fumadores o no-fumadores?
   (d) ¿Es un vuelo Londres-Madrid o Madrid-Londres?

—————————— **Diálogo 2** ——————————

Listen to (or read) this short dialogue between Isabel and
Ricardo.

Isabel	¿Qué quiere Vd. – un té o un café?
Ricardo	Quiero un café.
Isabel	¿Cómo lo quiere – solo o con leche?
Ricardo	Lo quiero con leche.
Isabel	¿Quiere azúcar?
Ricardo	No. No quiero azúcar.

¿Cómo lo quiere?	how do you want it?
lo quiero...	I want it ...
la leche	milk
el azúcar	sugar

Para estudiar

Lo/la quiero *I want it*

When instead of repeating the noun it is quicker and more natural
to substitute *it*, Spanish does this by inserting **lo** or **la**. Use **lo** if
the replaced word is masculine, and **la** if the replaced word is feminine. These become **los** and **las** (meaning *them*) when they re-
place plural words. Study the following examples:

Necesito un billete para Madrid.	*I need a ticket for Madrid.*
Lo necesito para viajar el día 19.	*I need it for travelling on the 19th.*
Tengo dos entradas de teatro. ¿Las quiere Vd.?	*I have two theatre tickets. Do you want them?*
Quisiera un té. Lo quisiera con limón.	*I'd like it with lemon.*

Actividad

3 Choose **lo, la, los** or **las** to fill the gaps in the sentences
below.
(a) ¿Cómo quiere Vd. el café – solo o con leche? ... quiero
solo.

(b) Quiero cuatro entradas de teatro. … quisiera para el jueves.

(c) Necesito dos billetes para Málaga. … quiero de ida y vuelta.

(d) ¿Cómo quiere Vd. el té – con leche o con limón? … quiero con limón.

(e) ¿Cómo quiere Vd. su aperitivo? … quisiera con mucha tónica y poco gin.

The language in this short unit is closely linked with that in the next. When you have checked your progress with the **Evaluación** below, go straight on to Unit 9.

Evaluación

Can you say the following in Spanish?
1 I'd like a coffee.
2 I need to be in Madrid on Friday.
3 Could you make a reservation, please?
4 I need to be in the office for a meeting on the 17th.
5 I'm going to Paris tomorrow. The flight leaves at 10.15am.
6 I'd like two theatre tickets for the 23rd, please.

9

GUSTOS Y PREFERENCIAS

Tastes and preferences

In this unit you will learn

- how to express a preference
- how to say what you like and dislike

Préambulo

I Me gusta … *I like …*

If you wish to say:
> *I like music*
> *I love Scotch whisky*
> *I adore the Spanish Pyrenees*

you say:
> **me gusta la música**
> **me gusta mucho el güisqui escocés**
> **me gusta muchísimo el Pirineo español**

In saying **me gusta la música** what you have in fact said is *music pleases me* and you can add **mucho** or **muchísimo** to express stronger degrees of liking. So *I like* is always **me gusta** or **me gustan**, according to whether you like one thing or more than one. For example:

Me gusta el té con limón.
Me gusta ir al cine.
Me gusta el arte de Picasso.
Me gustan los cafés de Madrid.
Me gustan los perros.
Me gustan todas las óperas de Verdi.

If you didn't like these things, you would say:

No me gusta el té con limon.
No me gusta la música de Verdi.
No me gustan los perros. etc.

La vida de los Méndez

Lectura

La señora Méndez habla su la vida en Madrid. *Mrs Méndez talks about her life in Madrid.* Read or listen twice to this description of the señores Méndez' life in Madrid. Pay special attention to how she talks about her own and her husband's likes and dislikes.

No me gusta la vida moderna. No me gusta vivir en Madrid. Hay demasiado tráfico. Hay demasiados coches en la calle. Quisiera vivir en Málaga pero mi marido no quiere. Mi marido se llama Benito. Benito Méndez Ortigosa. Quiero mucho a mi marido. Es un ángel. No tenemos mucho dinero pero estamos muy contentos. A mi marido le gusta vivir en Madrid. Dice que es más animado, más interesante. Le gusta ir al café con los amigos. Hablan de política y de fútbol. A mí me gusta ir al café para tomar un té o un chocolate. Me gusta también la televisión. Pero hay demasiada política y demasiado fútbol. Me gustan los seriales. A mi marido no le gustan. Dice que son demasiado sentimentales. Pero yo prefiero los seriales a la política.

la vida	life
el dinero	money
animado	lively
demasiado, demasiada	too, too much
demasiados, demasiadas	too many
preferir, prefiero	to prefer, I prefer

Comentario

A common way of expressing a contrast is:

A mí me gustan los seriales.	*I like serials.*
A mi marido no le gustan.	*My husband doesn't*
¿A Vd. le gusta la política?	*Do you like politics?*

The words a **mí**, **a mi marido**, **A Vd.** are not essential to the meaning, but are put in for emphasis.

Actividad

1 Fill in the gaps in the answers to the questions.
¿Qué dice la señora Méndez de Madrid?

(a) Dice que … … … vivir en Madrid.
¿Qué dice de Málaga?
(b) Dice que … vivir en Málaga.
¿Qué dice de su marido?
(c) Dice que le … mucho.
(d) Dice que … … Benito.
(e) Dice que es … … .
(f) Dice que … … vivir en Madrid.
¿Qué dice de ir a tomar chocolate?
(g) Dice que … … .
¿Qué dice de la televisión?
(h) Dice que hay … … .
¿Qué dice de los seriales en la televisión?
(i) Dice que … … .
¿Qué dice el señor Méndez de los seriales?
(j) Dice que … … … .
¿Le gustan al señor Méndez los seriales?
(k) No. No … … .

✳ Notice the word order of the last question. While the English is simpler *Does señor Méndez like (the) serials?* the Spanish literally means *to him/please/to señor Méndez/the serials?* where *to him* and *to señor Méndez* repeat the same thing. But you will notice this sort of repetition often in the latter part of the book. It is characteristic of Spanish. You have seen it already in **a mí me gusta** and **a mi marido le gusta**. Here **a mí** and **me, a mi marido** and **le** say the same thing twice to give emphasis and clarity.

Diálogos

Of course, even if you like something you don't always want it. Look at the following little dialogues:

Diálogo 1

Señor A ¿Quiere un café?
Señor B No, gracias.
Señor A ¿No le gusta?

Señor B   Sí, me gusta, pero no me apetece ahora.
Señor A   ¿Le apetece un aperitivo?
Señor B   Sí, me apetece un vermú.

Diálogo 2

Ricardo   ¿Quiere Vd. tomar algo?
Isabel   Sí. Gracias.
Ricardo   ¿Qué le apetece? ¿Güisqui, gin-tonic, vermú?
Isabel   No. No quiero alcohol. Me apetece un té, si lo hay.
Ricardo   ¿Lo prefiere con leche o limón?
Isabel   Prefiero té con leche, por favor.

apetecer (me apetece)	to appeal (lit. it appeals to me)
el vermú	vermouth
algo	something
si lo hay	if there is one/some

—— Para estudiar ——

1 Me apetece … *I feel like …*

Me apetece means *I feel like it* (lit. *it appeals to me*) and works in just the same way as **me gusta** in that it can be used with a noun or a verb.

No me apetece salir.	*I don't feel like going out.*
¿Le apetece un aperitivo?	*Do you feel like an aperitif?*
No le apetece trabajar hoy.	*He/she doesn't feel like working today.*
A mí no me apetece ir al cine, pero a mi amigo sí.	*I don't feel like going to the cinema, but my friend does.*

2 Prefiero… *I prefer…*

Notice that *to prefer* is **preferir**. *I prefer* and *he/she prefers/you prefer* are **prefiere**, or **Vd. prefiere**. The vowels **-ie-** appear instead of the **-e-** in the second syllable. *They prefer* is **prefieren**, but *we* *prefer* is **preferimos**, without the **-ie-**. This is a common pattern in Spanish – our new verb **quiero, quiere, quieren** but **queremos** (infinitive **querer**) behaves in exactly the same way. You will notice other examples of vowel changes, but just learn them as they occur.

☑ ———————— **Actividades** ————————

2 Speaking of coffee, can you:
  (a) say that you like it?
  (b) say that you prefer it with milk?
  (c) say that you don't want sugar?
  (d) say that you don't feel like one now?
  Speaking of tea, can you:
  (e) ask Isabel if she wants one?
  (f) ask her how she wants it?
  (g) ask her if she always prefers it with milk?
  (h) ask her if she doesn't like tea with sugar?
  Speaking of alcoholic drinks, can you:
  (i) ask Paco if he likes Spanish wines?
  (j) ask him if he prefers whisky or vermouth?
  (k) ask him if he feels like a gin and tonic?
  (l) ask him if he wants lemon in it?

3 You are in a thoroughly bad mood and don't feel like doing any of the things your friend suggests. Express your feelings as indicated in the square brackets after each question.
  (a) ¿Quiere ir al cine? [you don't feel like it]
  (b) ¡Vamos al café para tomar un chocolate! [you don't like chocolate]
  (c) ¿Prefiere Vd. un gin-tonic? [no, you don't want a gin and tonic]
  (d) ¿Quiere ir a la ópera? [you don't like Verdi's music]
  (e) ¿Prefiere salir en el coche? [you don't feel like it]
  (f) Entonces, ¿quiere Vd. ir a casa? [yes, you feel like going home]

4 Using the information in Señora Méndez's description of life
   in Madrid, imagine that you are Señor Méndez and match the
   phrases on the left with those on the right to make as many
   truthful sentences as you can.

(a) A mí no me gusta   (i)   hablar de fútbol.
(b) A mi mujer le gusta   (ii)   vivir en Madrid.
(c) A mí me gusta   (iii) el té.
(d) A mi mujer no le gusta   (iv)   el chocolate.
                              (v)   la vida moderna.
                              (vi)   la vida en Málaga.
                              (vii) un serial.
                              (viii) la política.

Documento número 8

```
*PARADOR DE TURISMO*
  NIF. A-79855201
IVA INCLUIDO*GRACIAS*
  *SALAMANCA*
  08-04-91 15:51
C001              131

4X            @155
CAFE          ·620
4X            @135
BOLLOS Y SIM  ·540
CAJA       -1-160
```

This cafe bill from the **Parador**
at Salamanca has a lot of
information. You can see the
date and time, and that VAT is
included. (Value Added Tax
is **IVA – Impuesto de Valor
Añadido**.) **Bollos y Sim(ilares)**
refers to the pastries that
we ate.

Try these questions:
(a) ¿Cuánto es un café?
(b) ¿Cuánto son cuatro cafés?
(c) ¿Para qué fecha es?
(d) ¿A qué hora?

☉ Sumario

Finally in this unit, here is a summary of this way of expressing your likes and dislikes (**gustar** and **apetecer** work in exactly the same way, so only **gustar** is given here). The examples below also include the *we* and *they* forms, which you have not used so far.

Me gusta el vino español.	*I like Spanish wine.*
Me gustan los vinos españoles.	*I like Spanish wines.*
Le gusta el viño español.	*He/she likes, you like Spanish wine.*
Le gustan los vinos españoles.	*He/she likes, you like Spanish wines.*
Nos gusta el vino español.	*We like Spanish wine.*
Nos gustan los vinos españoles.	*We like Spanish wines.*
Les gusta el vino español.	*They like Spanish wine.*
Les gustan los vinos españoles.	*They like Spanish wines.*

Remember that you can intensify what you are saying in this context by adding **mucho** or **muchísimo**.

It helps to know that what you are really saying is that Spanish wine or wines please me/him/her/you/us/them. Liking things is always expressed in this way (or disliking, if you place **no** in front). It is very easy once you have practised it a little. The same idea lies behind other phrases which you will come across later.

✼ One final point – if you are offered a choice but you have no particular preference, you can say

Me da igual.   *It's all the same to me.*

☑ Evaluación

Can you do the following?
1 Say you like music.
2 Say you like flamenco music very much.
3 Say you do not like football.
4 Say you prefer classical music (**la música clásica**).
5 Ask a friend if he/she likes flamenco.
6 Ask a friend if he/she prefers flamenco or classical.

7 Say you want to go home because you don't feel like doing any more work and you need a gin and tonic.

Documento número 9

A travel agency is advertising some cheap flights (**a precios de auténtica ganga**, *at real bargain prices*).

Try the questions:
- (a) ¿Quiere Vd. ir a Mallorca? (*Say no, you don't*)
- (b) ¿O prefiere ir a Gran Canaria? (*Say yes, you do*)
- (c) ¿Cuánto cuesta ir a las islas Baleares?
- (d) ¿Y cuánto a las Canarias?
- (e) ¿Dónde necesita hacer la reserva?

10

COSAS PERSONALES
Personal matters

In this unit you will learn

- how to talk about personal activities such as washing and dressing
- how to make impersonal statements about people in general

Preámbulo

Many of the things we do reflect on ourselves i.e. they are personal activities, such as getting up, going to bed, washing, dressing, sitting down, as well as personal feelings such as enjoying oneself, or feeling ill or well. In these cases, Spanish uses the little words **me** (*myself*), **se** (*himself, herself, yourself/yourselves*), and **nos** (*ourselves*) together with the verb expressing the action or state. The little words used in this way are called 'reflexive pronouns'. You have already seen an example in **me llamo** *my name is* (lit. *I call myself*). Other examples are:

me lavo	*I wash (myself)*
me levanto	*I get up*
me siento bien	*I feel well*

Paco **se levanta** a las siete. *Paco gets up at seven.*
Le señora Méndez siempre   *Mrs Méndez always feels*
   se siente bien en Málaga.   *well in Málaga.*
Nos divertimos mucho   *We enjoy ourselves a lot*
   cuando estamos de   *when we are on holiday.*
   vacaciones.

Notice the difference between:

Lavo el coche todos los domingos. *I wash the car on*
and   *Sundays.*
Me lavo todos los días.   *I wash (i.e. myself)*
                                           every day.

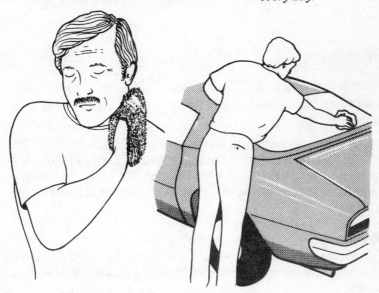

Monólogos

Monólogo 1

Isabel habla de lo que Paco hace todas las mañanas. *Isabel describes what Paco does every morning.*

Paco se levanta a las siete. Se lava y se viste y sale de casa a las ocho menos veinte. Va en coche a la oficina. Llega a las ocho, y se sienta inmediatamente para trabajar. Le gusta su trabajo. Tiene compañeros simpáticos y se siente bien en el ambiente de la oficina.

⚬ Comentario

Se viste means *he dresses*. **El ambiente** means *the atmosphere* or *the environment*. Notice **se siente**, *he feels*, and **se sienta**, *he sits down*. The two verbs are very alike. **Me siento** can mean *I feel* or *I sit*. The first is from **sentir**, *to feel*, and the second from **sentar**, *to seat* or *sit*.

▤ Monólogo 2

Now Paco gives you the same information, speaking for himself. Notice how the verbs change – they will end in **-o**, of course (see Unit 8).

Me levanto a las siete. Me lavo y me visto y salgo de casa a las ocho menos veinte. Voy en coche a la oficina. Llego a las ocho, y me siento inmediatamente para trabajar. Me gusta mi trabajo. Tengo compañeros simpáticos y me siento bien en el ambiente de la oficina.

▤ Monólogo 3

Now Señora Méndez describes her morning routine and her husband's:

Benito y yo nos levantamos tarde. No tenemos prisa porque mi marido está jubilado y no trabaja. Nos lavamos y nos vestimos y salimos a la calle a las doce. Vamos al café y nos sentamos en la terraza. Nos gusta salir todos los días.

⚬ Comentario

Tener prisa means *to be in a hurry*. **No tenemos prisa** is *we're not in a hurry*. Benito Méndez is retired (**jubilado**). Instead of

— 90 —

saying **nos lavamos y nos vestimos**, Señora Méndez could have said **nos arreglamos**, *we get ready*. **Arreglar** is *to arrange*. If you want to use it in the special sense of *to arrange oneself*, or *get ready*, you would call the verb **arreglarse**. You put -**se** on the end of an infinitive to show it is being used in this 'reflective' way. **Hablar** is *to speak*; **hablarse** is *to talk to yourself!*

——————— Actividad ———————

1   Answer these questions on the above little monologues:
   (a) ¿Qué hace Paco a las siete?
   (b) ¿Y qué hace inmediatamente después?
   (c) ¿A qué hora sale de casa?
   (d) ¿Qué hace cuando llega a la oficina a las ocho?
   (e) ¿Por qué se siente bien en el ambiente de la oficina?
   (f) ¿Los Méndez se levantan a las siete?
   (g) ¿Por qué no?
   (h) ¿Qué hacen antes de salir? (**antes de**, *before*)
   (i) ¿Qué hacen cuando llegan al café?
   (j) ¿Qué dice la señora de salir todos los días?

——————Para estudiar ——————

Se, *one*

Another helpful use of the little word **se** is when you are talking about people in general. (See also Unit 6). For example you might want to say:

In Spain, one says 'buenos días'.
or   In Spain, you (you in general) say 'buenos días'.
or   In Spain, they (i.e. people in general) say 'buenos días'.
All these are translated by:
En España, **se dice** 'buenos días'.
You have seen this sort of phrase before in:
Se habla español.   *One speaks Spanish/Spanish spoken.*

and in   **Se puede ... ?**   *May one ... ? or may I ... ?*

Notice the invaluable question

| **¿Cómo se dice ... en español?** | *How do you say ... in Spanish?* |

Several verbs can be used in this way to ask about what is generally done. Here are some more examples:

En Inglaterra, **se bebe** más té que café.	*In England, they drink more coffee than tea.*
En España, **se bebe** más café que té.	*In Spain, they drink more coffee than tea.*
En Inglaterra, se paga en libras esterlinas.	*In England, one pays in pounds sterling.*
En España, **se paga** en pesetas.	*In Spain, one pays in pesetas.*
En Inglaterra, **se circula** por la izquierda.	*In England, you drive on the left.*
En España, **se circula** por la derecha.	*In Spain, you drive on the right.*
Notice: **por la derecha**	*on the right*
por la izquierda	*on the left*

Notice also **más ... que**, *more ... than*. This invaluable little word **que** can mean *who*, *which*, *that* or *than*, and in a question **¿qué?** can mean *which?* or *what?*. **Que** cannot be omitted like *which* or *that* in English:

El libro **que** tengo ...   The book (which/that) I have ...

☑ ─────── **Actividades** ───────

2   Look again at the descriptions of what Paco and Señora Méndez do every morning. Here are the answers they give to your questions. What did you ask them?
    (a) Paco: Me levanto a las siete.
    (b) Paco: A las ocho menos veinte.

(c) Paco: Llego a las ocho.

(d) Paco: Sí. Me gusta.

(e) Paco: Porque tengo compañeros simpáticos.

(f) Sra. Méndez: Nos levantamos muy tarde.

(g) Sra. Méndez: Porque mi marido no trabaja.

(h) Sra. Méndez: Porque está jubilado.

(i) Sra. Méndez: A las doce.

(j) Sra. Méndez: En la terraza.

3 Choose one of the phrases on the right to complete each of the sentences started on the left.

(a) En España, se circula
  (i) en la terraza.
  (ii) por la derecha.
  (iii) a las doce.

(b) En Cataluña,
  (i) les gusta el té.
  (ii) no se entiende catalán.
  (iii) viven los catalanes.

(c) A las siete de la tarde
  (i) me lavo.
  (ii) salgo de la oficina.
  (iii) me visto.

(d) Los señores Méndez se levantan
  (i) tarde.
  (ii) en la oficina.
  (iii) después de vestirse.

(e) Paco se siente bien en la oficina porque
  (i) le gusta sentarse.
  (ii) no le apetece el trabajo.
  (iii) tiene compañeros simpáticos.

(f) Cuando los señores Méndez van al café
  (i) beben un güisqui.
  (ii) toman un chocolate.
  (iii) llegan a las cuatro.

4 Use **se** verbs to say that:

(a) One has an aperitive at 7pm.

(b) One eats well in Spain.

(c) They speak Spanish well in Burgos.

(d) People feel happier at home than in the office.

(e) One needs to work a lot.

(f) One goes out with the dog every day.

(g) You may not pay by cheque.

(h) In England, people drink more tea than wine.

Documento número 10

**IMPORTANTE EMPRESA
DE INFORMATICA
S o l i c i t a**

RECEPCIONISTA

**Se ocupará también de
ciertas labores
de Secretariado**

Se requiere:

- Imprescindible inglés y/o
  francés para atender llamadas telefónicas en di-
  chos·idiomas.
- Experiencia en manejo de
  máquina y mejor con cono-
  cimientos de tratamiento
  de textos sobre PC.
- Edad desde 18 a 25 años.

Se ofrece:

- Contrato laboral.
- Incorporación inmediata.
- Horario de 8,30 a 13,30 y
  de 14,30 a 17,30.

**Escribir urgentemente al
apartado 6102,
28080 MADRID,
adjuntando
Curriculum Vitae con
fotografía
(imprescindible),
e indicando
pretensiones económicas.
Ref. RECEPCIONISTA/6.**

Look at this job advertisement for a receptionist in a computer company (*computing* is **informática**). Notice **se ocupará**, *she will occupy herself* (secretarial work is also required) and **se requiere**, *one requires* (they want English and/or French with typing or preferably word-processing skills) and **se ofrece**, *one offers*. In the address, **apartado 6102** is a post office box number.

What three things will the company offer someone with these skills?

☑ Evaluación

Can you do the following in Spanish?
1 Say Paco is in a hurry.
2 Say we are in a hurry.

3   Say you get dressed at 7am and go out at 8.30.
4   Say that you have a good time on Saturdays.
5   Say you don't feel well, you want to return home.
6   Ask if it's possible to pay with a credit card.
7   Say that you get up late every Sunday.
8   Say that don't like working in the office, because your colleagues are unpleasant.

11

ENTRE AMIGOS
Between friends

In this unit you will learn

- how to say *you* when talking to family and friends

Preámbulo

So far in this book, in talking to another person, we have used the forms **Vd. (usted)** and **Vds. (ustedes)** for *you*. But Spanish, in common with French, German, Italian and other languages (but not English) has more than one way of saying *you*. If you know a person well, or if you want to talk to them informally, you address them as **tú**, not **Vd.**. **Tú** is used among members of a family, between friends, when talking to children, and among young people generally. Its use is spreading as the old formality of Spanish life gives place to a more relaxed style. Adults meeting each other for the first time in a private social function will often address each other as **tú**. So it is sometimes difficult to know whether to use **tú** to a Spanish acquaintance or **Vd.** If in doubt, keep to **Vd.** until your Spanish friend uses **tú**. It is better to be thought too formal than too familiar, which is why we have started off by using **Vd.** But you may hear a much greater use of **tú** in Spain, if not in South and Central America, depending on the social and age groups you are mixing within.

This unit will give you some practice in the use of **tú** (and its plural **vosotros**). We shall do this by means of re-working some of the material we have had in previous units, which will at the same time give you some useful revision before you move on to the second part of the book.

Para estudiar

1 Comparing Vd. and tú

Listen to, or read through, the following short exchanges, which we have adapted as necessary from dialogues you have already seen. Henceforward it will be natural, as they are young people, to talk to Paco and Isabel as **tú**, (or jointly as **vosotros**). The señores Méndez, however, are an older and more old-fashioned couple, so it will be more appropriate to continue to use **Vd.** and **Vds.** when talking to them.

From unit 1

¿Quién es Vd?	Soy el señor Méndez.
¿Quién eres (tú)?	Soy Paco.
¿Eres Luisa?	No. No soy Luisa.
¿Cómo te llamas, pues?	Me llamo Isabel.

From unit 2

¿De dónde eres, Paco?	Soy de Madrid.
¿De dónde eres, Isabel?	Soy de Madrid.
¿De dónde sois, Isabel y Paco?	Somos de Madrid.

From unit 3

¿Dónde vives, Isabel?	Vivo en la calle Almagro.
¿Y dónde trabajas?	Trabajo en la calle María de Molina.

2 Vd. es and tú eres

Notice that if you are talking to someone as **Vd.**, you use:

es
vive
trabaja

---

but when addressing them as **tú**, you use:

eres
vives
trabajas

The forms used with **tú** always end in **-s**. More examples:

From unit 4

¿Cómo está Vd., doña Aurora? | Estoy bien, gracias, ¿y Vd?
Hola, Paco. ¿Cómo estás? | Estoy bien, gracias, ¿y tú?
¿Estás de vacaciones? | Todavía no. Voy en julio.

From unit 5

Isabel, ¿cuántos hermanos
tienes? | Tengo una hermana y dos
hermanos.
Paco, ¿dónde tienes tu coche? | Está en la calle. No tengo
garage.

Isabel, ¿tienes un coche para ti
sola? | No. A mí gustan los taxis.

From unit 6

¿Cuándo vas a Santander, Paco? | Voy el 5 de junio.
¿Y cuándo vuelves a Madrid? | Vuelve el 10 de junio.

3 Tu *and* ti

You will notice that when using **tú** to Paco or Isabel we also have to say **tu coche** (*your car*) and **para ti sola** (*for you alone*).

4 Vosotros sois

In all the above, we have been addressing Paco or Isabel as **tú**. Look again at the verb forms we have been using. But when we asked them jointly where they were from, we said:

¿De dónde sois, Isabel y Paco?

You use **sois** when talking to two people, or a group of people, with all of whom you are familiar. The word for *you* in this case is **vosotros**, replacing **Vds.**. Look again at **Actividad 4** in Unit 6, where we asked questions of the Méndez couple. If we knew them well enough to use familiar forms of address, we should ask:

¿Por qué estáis en Málaga?
¿Cuándo volvéis a Madrid?
¿Cuánto tiempo pasáis en Malaga?
¿Estáis en un hotel?
¿Dónde vais hoy para tomar el aperitivo?
¿También coméis en el café?
¿Tenéis familia en Málaga?
¿Qué hacéis después de la siesta si no visitáis a amigos?

Read the above again, and compare with the earlier version, noting the changes we have had to make in switching from **Vds.** to **vosotros**. You need not spend a lot of time learning these yet, as most conversations are one-to-one, rather than to pairs or groups. Concentrate on the **tú** forms for the present.

From unit 8

¿Qué quieres – un té o un café?   Quiero un café.
¿Cómo lo quieres – con leche?   No. Lo quiero solo.

5   I love you

Remember that **quiero**, used of people, means *I love*. Naturally you use the familiar form when telling someon you love him/her.

¿Me quieres?   Sí. Te quiero.
¿Cuánto me quieres?   Te quiero muchísimo. Te
                           adoro.

and so on.

6   Te gusta?

From unit 9

If you want to ask a friend whether he/she likes something, you say:

¿Te gusta el arte de Picasso?
¿Te gustan las óperas de Verdi?

or whether he/she has a preference:

¿Qué prefieres – vino blanco o vino tinto?
¿Te apetece un vino ahora?

No gracias. No me apetece en este memento.

🔲 *From unit 10*
¿A qué hora te levantas, Paco?
Me levanto a las siete.
¿Te lavas todos los días?
Naturalmente.
¿A qué hora sales de casa?
Salgo a las ocho menos veinte.
¿Tienes prisa? ¿Por qué no te sientas un poco? (*Are you in a hurry? Why don't you sit down for a bit?*)

Notice that when you are talking to someone as **tú**, you use **te gusta** instead of **le gusta**, and **te levantas** instead of **se levanta**. There will be much more practice on talking to people using **tú** in the second part of the book, where, as you will see, we shall use both the formal and informal mode of address according to whatever the relationship is between the speakers.

🔲 ——————— **Actividad** ———————

Here are some questions addressed to Señor and/or Señora Méndez. Repeat the questions using **tú** or **vosotros** to Paco and Isabel.
  (a) Señor Méndez, es Vd. madrileño, ¿no?
  (b) ¿Va Vd. todos los días al café, señor?
  (c) ¿Tiene Vd. un coche, señor?
  (d) ¿Le gusta el fútbol, señor Méndez?
  (e) ¿Tiene Vd. prisa por las mañanas, señor?
  (f) Señora Méndez, ¿dónde pasa Vd. sus vacaciones?
  (g) Y ¿dónde prefiere Vd. vivir?
  (h) ¿Qué le apetece más, señora, un té o un café?
  (i) ¿Qué familia tienen Vds., señores?
  (j) ¿A qué hora salen Vds. por la mañana, señores?

✳ In the last two questions, you can say **Isabel y Paco**. But the other way round you have to say **Paco e Isabel**. The little word **y** changes to **e** when the next word begins with an **i-**. For example you say **Inglaterra y Espana**, but **Espana e Inglaterra**, and **hablo italiano y francés**, but **hablo francés e italiano**.

—— **100** ——

We will not have an **Evaluación** in this unit, as there has been an element of revision in the examples we have given you. This is the last of the basic units. If you have safely reached this point – well done! We hope you have enjoyed the course so far, and feel that you have begun to acquire a basic competence in Spanish. If you feel reasonably confident that you have understood and remembered what we have covered in the first eleven units, now tackle the next ten. You can look at units 12 to 20 in any order (21 is a summing-up) but unless you have good reasons for doing otherwise it's probably best to take them in the order they appear.

12

DÉSE A CONOCER

Make yourself known

In this unit you will learn

- how to give official details (passports, driving licences, etc.)
- the rest of the numbers

Preámbulo

To give information about yourself you need to be secure in your use of numbers, and to be able to spell words using the Spanish alphabet. Look back at the Introduction and practise saying the names of the letters in Spanish. (They are also on the tape.) Then practise spelling your name, and the name of the road, street or town where you live. (The question you will hear when you are asked to spell something is **¿Cómo se escribe?** *How do you write it?*)

Revise numbers in the first part of this book, as follows.
   Numbers 1– 20: Unit 3

Numbers 21–31 : Unit 6
Numbers 32–199: Unit 7

The plural hundreds are:

200	doscientos	600	seiscientos
300	trescientos	700	setecientos
400	cuatrocientos	800	ochocientos
500	quinientos	900	novecientos

Notice particularly the words for 500, 700 and 900.

When you are talking about numbers of things, including amounts of money, the multiple hundred numbers (**doscientos**, **trescientos**, etc.) will end in **-as** if what you are talking about is feminine. For example:

500 pts. quinient*as* pesetas   £600 seiscient*as* libras
but
DM 400 cuatrocient*os* marcos   FF 900 novecient*os* francos

As you know, *one thousand* is **mil**, *two thousand* **dos mil**.

So if you want a long number, such as the the date we saw in Unit 7, you just string all the words together, remembering to insert **y** (*and*) between any tens and units. For example:

1997	mil novecientos noventa y siete
1588	mil quinientos ochenta y ocho
16,000	dieciséis mil
237,741	doscientos treinta y siete mil, setecientos cuarenta y uno.

You are not likely to need many long numbers such as the last one. Being able to name recent and future years, however, can be very useful.

While we are thinking about numbers, remember how to give a telephone number; this was mentioned briefly in Unit 4. You say them in pairs, starting with the single digit if there is an odd number of figures. For example:

222069	veintidós, veinte, sesenta y nueve
760645	setenta y seis, cero seis, cuarenta y cinco
4452962	cuatro, cuarenta y cinco, veintinueve, sesenta y dos

⚽ **Comentario**

Paco arrives at the hotel where he is to stay in Santander for the conference. He is asked to complete a registration card. Study the card before reading the **Comentario** below.

Nombre ....

Apellidos ....

.... Fecha de nacimiento.............

Dirección ....

....

Nacionalidad .... DNI N° / ....

Expedido en .... Fecha ....

The first requirement is Paco's first or christian name; **nombre** can mean name in general, or first name in particular. **Apellidos** are surnames (remember the Spanish have two). He then has to give his date of birth, address, nationality and identity card number, and the place and date of its issue. **DNI** stands for **Documento Nacional de Identidad**, the identity card all Spaniards have. It is popularly called **el carnet** (or *el carné*).

❊ A tip – when making, say, a hotel reservation, it's best not to give more than one first, or Christian, name with your surname. As the Spanish are used to two surnames it might be assumed that your second Christian name is your first surname. If your reservation appears to be lost always check under your Christian names.

Actividad

1 See if you can answer the following questions, as they apply to yourself. We cannot give the answers to these in the **Clave**, of course.
   (a) ¿Cuál es su apellido?
   (b) ¿Cómo se escribe?
   (c) ¿Dónde vive Vd.?
   (d) ¿Y su dirección exacta?
   (e) ¿Tiene Vd. número de teléfono?
   (f) ¿Cuál es su fecha de nacimiento?
   (g) ¿Tiene Vd. pasaporte y carnet, o solamente pasaporte?
   (h) ¿Qué nacionalidad tiene Vd?

Diálogos

Listen to the following short conversations if you have the tape, and practise reading them aloud, especially the numbers.

Diálogo 1

¿Tiene Vd. permiso de conducir?
Sí, tengo.
¿Qué número tiene?
Es el OP64302.
¿Cuál es la fecha de caducidad?
El cuatro de septiembre, del año 2022.

Diálogo 2

¿Usa Vd. tarjeta de crédito? (Visa, Access?)
Sí, claro.
¿Qué es el número de la tarjeta?
Es el 21436580.
¿En qué fecha caduca?
Caduca el dos de mayo, de 1995.

Diálogo 3

¿Tiene Vd. seguro de accidente?
Sí, tengo.
¿Cuál es el número de la poliza?
El número de la poliza es FL6724.

Diálogo 4

¿Tiene Vd. cheques de viajero?
Sí, tengo.
¿Cuántos cheques tiene?
Tengo diez cheques.
¿Son en dólares o en libras esterlinas?
Son en dólares.
¿Qué valor tienen en total?
Dos mil dólares.

permiso de conducir	driving licence
fecha de caducidad	expiry date
caduca	it expires
tarjeta	card
seguro	insurance
poliza	policy

 ———————————**Actividad**———————————

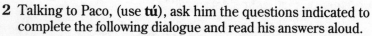

2 Talking to Paco, (use **tú**), ask him the questions indicated to complete the following dialogue and read his answers aloud.

(a) *You*   *Ask if he has an identity card.*
Paco   Sí, tengo, naturalmente, como todas los españoles.
(b) *You*   *Ask what the number is.*
Paco   Es el 4.768.905
(c) *You*   *Ask when it expires.*
Paco   Caduca el 7 de octubre, de 1998. Los carnet caducan a los diez años.

(d) *You*   *Ask whether he has a driving licence.*
Paco   Sí, aquí está.
(e) *You*   *Ask whether he has a passport.*
Paco   Sí, tengo, pero caduca este año.
(f) *You*   *Ask if he uses a credit card.*
Paco   Sí, una tarjeta Visa.
(g) *You*   *Ask if he is insured?*
Paco   Sí, desde luego (*of course*).
(h) *You*   *Ask what his insurance policy number is.*
Paco   Es el 2040648.
(i) *You*   *Ask where he lives.*
Paco   En la calle Meléndez Valdés 5, 3°D.
(j) *You*   *Ask for his telephone number.*
Paco   Es el 2253819.
(k) *You*   *Ask what his surnames are.*
Paco   Son Ruiz Gallego; me llamo Francisco Ruiz Gallego.
(l) *You*   *Ask how they are spelt.*
Paco   Se escriben R-U-I-Z G-A-L-L-E-G-O.

3 Isabel has lost her purse while visiting a friend in Bilbao. She goes to the police station and is asked for various personal details. Match her answers, given on the right, with the questions given on the left.

(a) ¿Sus apellidos, por favor?   (i) Aquí lo tiene.
(b) ¿Y su nombre?   (ii) El doce de mayo, 1970
(c) ¿Dónde vive Vd.?
(d) ¿Su fecha de nacimiento?   (iii) Isabel
(e) ¿Su carnet, por favor?   (iv) El día 20
(f) ¿Cuándo vuelve Vd. a Madrid?   (v) Ballester García
    (vi) Almagro 14, 6°A, Madrid

4 Say the following prices, and telephone numbers and years aloud.

(a) 500 pesetas   (g) 200 pesetas
(b) 1.238 pesetas   (h) 1995
(c) 164 pesetas   (i) 1984
(d) 100 pesetas   (j) 2010
(e) 2500 pesetas   (k) tel. 64910
(f) 50,000 pesetas   (l) tel. 487326

Documento número 11

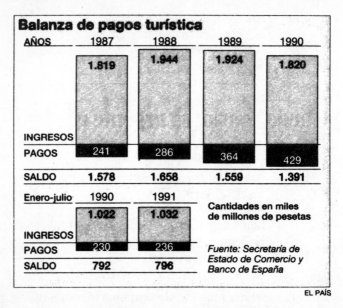

Balanza de pagos turística

AÑOS	1987	1988	1989	1990
INGRESOS	1.819	1.944	1.924	1.820
PAGOS	241	286	364	429
SALDO	1.578	1.658	1.559	1.391

Enero-julio	1990	1991
INGRESOS	1.022	1.032
PAGOS	230	236
SALDO	792	796

Cantidades en miles de millones de pesetas

Fuente: Secretaría de Estado de Comercio y Banco de España

EL PAÍS

Here is a record of Spain's earnings from the tourist industry. **Ingresos** is *income*, **pagos**, *expenditure*, and **saldo**, *balance*. As you can see, there was a decline in the late '80s. Practise reading the numbers aloud in Spanish and then answer the questions below the table.

(a) Figures are given for which months in particular of 1990 and 1991?

(b) How many noughts should be added to each figure in the table?

Evaluación

Can you say the following?

1 My date of birth is …
2 My surname is …
3 My address is …
4 My passport number is …
5 I am insured – the policy number is …
6 I'd like to pay with a credit card.

13

EN CASA
At home

In this unit you will learn

- how to talk about Spanish homes
- vocabulary useful for renting accommodation in Spain

¿Cómo es su casa?
What's your house like?

—————— Lectura ——————

Isabel describe el piso donde vive con su familia. *Isabel describes the flat where she lives with her family.*

Listen to Isabel's description (or read it) twice, referring to the vocabulary list for words that you cannot guess.

Como ya saben Vds., vivo en la calle Almagro, número 14. Vivo con mis padres. Somos cuatro hermanos, pero mi hermana Margarita está casada y vive con su marido Luis. Así que viven cinco adultos en mi casa. Menos mal que es bastante grande. Tenemos cuatro dormitorios, un salón, un comedor y un pequeño cuarto de estar. Hay dos cuartos de baño y la cocina tiene al lado otro cuarto pequeño para lavar y planchar. Aunque la casa es vieja, tenemos calefacción central y todas las habitaciones son grandes, con techos altos. El salón y dos dormitorios son exteriores y tienen balcones a la calle. Los demás cuartos dan a un patio bastante amplio, así que el piso tiene mucha luz. Me gusta mucho la casa, y también el barrio donde está.

From now on the lists of key words and phrases will always give verbs in the infinitive, nouns in the singular and adjectives in the masculine singular as you would find them in a dictionary.

ya	already
saber	to know
así que	so
menos mal que	it's just as well that
bastante	fairly, reasonably
el dormitorio	bedroom
el salón	sitting room
el comedor	dining room
el cuarto de estar	living room
el cuarto de baño	bathroom
la cocina	kitchen
el lado	side
planchar	to iron, press
aunque	although
viejo	old
la calefacción	heating
la habitación	room
el techo	ceiling
alto	high
exterior	outside (i.e. on the frontage of the building)
los demás	the rest, the others
dar a	look on to
amplio	ample, spacious
la luz	light
el barrio	district

Now Paco describes his flat.

Vivo en un piso moderno alquilado en la calle Meléndez Valdés, de Madrid. Es muy pequeño – es más apartamento que piso. Tiene un dormitorio, un salón, una cocina y un cuarto de baño. Las habitaciones son todas pequeñas – el piso no es apto para una familia. Pero para mí es muy práctico porque está ideado para personas profesionales. La cocina está muy bien instalada con nevera, lavadora y fregaplatos. También hay un horno micro-ondas. Hay instalación de aire acondicionado y video-portero. Me arreglo muy bien allí.

apto	suitable
ideado	designed
instalada	equipped
la nevera	fridge
la lavadora	washing machine
el fregaplatos	dishwasher
el horno micro-ondas	microwave oven
instalación de aire acondicionada	air-conditioning
video-portero	video entryphone
arreglarse	to manage (*also* to dress, get ready)
allí	there

Comentario

The word **casa** can be used to denote *home*, whether home is a house or a flat. For example

| **Me voy a casa.** | *I'm going home.* |
| **Paco no está en casa.** | *Paco is not at home.* |

It can also describe a building containing flats. For example:

| **Es una casa moderna de diez plantas.** | *It's a modern ten-storey block.* |

or it can be a house in the normal sense, i.e. a two- or three- storey building with single occupancy. A modern detached house in the country or on the coast is usually **un chalet** (pronounced as in English) and a semi-detached house **un chalet adosado**. As we have seen, **apartamento** is used for a small flat, and the fashionable term for a one-room flat is **un estudio** corresponding to the English studio flat.

☑ ─────────── **Actividades** ───────────

In this unit we have a role-play exercise. Imagine you are trying to rent accommodation for a month's holiday. You go to the *Agencia Solymar*, which is somewhere on the Costa Blanca. Read what the employee of the agency says, and supply the missing lines. See how far you can do before you look at Diálogo 2, where the roles are reversed. Go right through to the end of Diálogo 1 without giving up – miss out lines that you can't manage.

Diálogo 1

Empleado	Buenos días. ¿En qué puedo servirle?
You	*Say you want to rent a villa or a flat for the month of August.*
Empleado	Nos queda muy poco para agosto. ¿Para cuántas personas es?
You	*Say it's only for two people. You would like a house with a garden.*
Empleado	Tengo dos chalets, pero son grandes, con cuatro dormitorios.
You	*Say they are too big.*
Empleado	Para dos personas tengo un apartamento solamente.
You	*Ask if it's near the beach.*
Empleado	No muy cerca. Está en el centro. Es muy conveniente para todo.
You	*Ask for more details.*
Empleado	Aquí tiene Vd. un plano. Salón-comedor, cuarto de baño, cocina. El salón tiene un sofá y dos butacas, y el dormitorio cama de matrimonio.

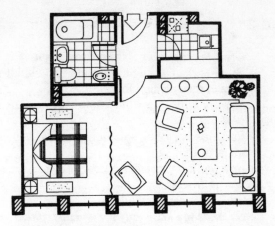

You	*Ask what floor it's on.*
Empleado	La cuarta. Es una casa moderna. Tiene mucha luz.
You	*Ask if there is a refrigerator in the kitchen.*
Empleado	Sí. Una nevera grande, y cocina de gas butano.
You	*Ask what is in the bathroom.*
Empleado	Un baño con ducha, lavabo, water y bidet. Hay agua caliente de la casa.
You	*Ask if there is air conditioning.*
Expleado	No. Pero el piso es exterior y está muy bien ventilado.
You	*Assume there is a television.*
Empleado	Sí. La casa tiene antena parabólica. Recibe todos los canales.
You	*Ask what the rent is.*
Empleado	Setenta y dos mil pesetas al mes, pago por adelantado.
You	*Thank him. You will think it over.*

Some of the Spanish in **Diálogo** 1 may well have stumped you. So here is the same dialogue again, with the languages reversed. This time try to supply what the employee of the Agencia Solymar says, and note what you might have said in **Diálogo 1**. See how much you can do without looking back.

Diálogo 2

You	*Greet the customer. Ask how you can help.*
Cliente	Buenos días. Quisiera alquilar un chalet o un piso para el mes de agosto.
You	*Say you have very little left for August. Ask how many people it's for.*
Cliente	Para dos personas solamente. Quisiera una casa con un jardín.
You	*Say you have two villas, but they are big ones, with four bedrooms.*
Cliente	Son demasiado grandes.
You	*Say that you have only got one apartment for two people.*
Cliente	¿Está cerca de la playa?
You	*Say that it is not very near. But it is in the centre, and very convenient for everything.*
Cliente	¿Tiene más detalles?
You	*Say, here is a plan. Sitting room, bedroom, bathroom, kitchen. The sitting room has a sofa and two armchairs. There is a double bed in the bedroom.*
Cliente	¿En qué planta está?
You	*Say on the fourth. It's a modern house, and it's very light.*
Cliente	¿Hay una nevera en la cocina?
You	*Say yes. A large refrigerator, and a calor gas cooker.*
Cliente	¿Qué hay en el cuarto de baño?
You	*A bath with a shower, a washbasin, a lavatory and a bidet. The house has a mains hot water supply.*
Cliente	¿Hay aire acondicionado?
You	*No. but the flat is on the outside of the building and is well ventilated.*
Cliente	Hay una televisión, ¿verdad?
You	*Yes. Say the house has a dish aerial and can receive all the channels.*
Cliente	Cuánto es el alquiler?
You	*Say seventy–two thousand pesetas a month, payable in advance.*
Cliente	Muchas gracias. Lo voy a pensar.

Repeat both the exercises until you can do each without referring to the other.

Documento número 12

MARBELLA
WHITE PEARL BEACH

Apartamentos de lujo en primera linea de playa, justo al lado del Hotel Don Carlos, le ofrecen un estilo de vida exclusivo en un marco ambiental creado para satisfacer al gusto más exigente.

Oportunidad unica de inversión con ofertas de hasta un 30% de descuento.

Para mayor información, llámenos ahora al teléfono
(952) 830955 / 832230
Fax (952) 831781
Oficina de ventas abierta
de 10.00 a 21.00 horas.

ACCEPTING ALL CHALLENGE

Lovell España

An advertisement for some luxury apartments, designed to satisfy the most demanding tastes. They are an investment opportunity with up to 30% discounts available. How far from the beach are they?

14

USEMOS EL TIEMPO LIBRE
Free time activities

In this unit you will learn

● how to talk about things to do and places to visit

¿Qué hace en su tiempo libre?
What do you do in your free time?

Lectura

Vamos a preguntar a Paco lo que hace en su tiempo libre. *Let's ask Paco what he does in his free time.*

Listen to or read Paco's description of his leisure time; see how much you can understand before you refer to the following vocabulary list. Then do the same with what Isabel and Señor Méndez say.

Como paso mucho tiempo en la oficina sentado, me gusta hacer ejercicio para estar en forma. Hay un gimnasio cerca de mi casa y voy allí dos veces por semana cuando tengo tiempo. Los fines de semana en verano juego al tenis con amigos o vamos todos a la piscina para nadar. En invierno juego al squash en el gimnasio. No veo mucho la televisión pero me gusta ir al cine o al teatro. No puedo salir todas las tardes porque a veces tengo trabajo para un cliente particular que hago en casa. Mis padres viven en Alicante y siempre voy allí para las vacaciones. Durante el mes de agosto no hago nada sino comer, beber, nadar y tomar el sol. ¡Es estupendo!

sentado	seated, sitting
estar en forma	keep fit
dos veces por semana	twice a week
el fin de semana	weekend
el verano	summer
jugar a	play (sports)
la piscina	swimming pool
ver	see, watch
a veces	sometimes
particular	private (*i.e. not* particular)
siempre	always
durante	during
no hago nado sino ...	I do nothing but ...
nadar	swim
estupendo	marvellous

Ahora, vamos a preguntar a Isabel cómo ella pasa el tiempo libre. Yo no hago ningún deporte. No me interesa mucho. Prefiero la música. Me gusta muchísimo la música. Toco un poco el piano y la guitarra y voy a muchos conciertos. A veces salgo con Paco y otros amigos al teatro o al cine. También voy a museos y galerías cuando hay una exposición especial.
Y ¿qué deporte hace Vd., señor Méndez?

ningún deporte	any sport at all
tocar	play (music, instrument)
la galería	gallery
la exposición	exhibition

¡Uf! Yo no hago deporte ahora. Soy demasiado viejo. Pero me gusta el fútbol. Cuando hay un partido en la televisión siempre lo veo; sobre todo cuando juega el Atlético de Madrid. Y cuando ponen la Copa de Europa o la Copa Mundial me lo paso muy bien. Mi señora y yo vamos al teatro de vez en cuando. Nos gustan las zarzuelas que ponen en el Teatro de la Villa. Pero salimos poco, salvo al café.

el partido	match
sobre todo	above all
poner	put (on)
me lo paso muy bien	I enjoy it very much
de vez en cuando	occasionally, sometimes
la zarzuela	Spanish operetta
salvo	except

Actividad

1 Fill in the blanks to complete the answers to the following questions.

Isabel y el señor Méndez no hacen deporte. ¿Por qué no?

(a)   A Isabel................. El señor Méndez ....

¿Qué cosas les gustan?

(b)   A Isabel................. Al señor Méndez ....

¿Cómo sabemos que les gusta la música o el fútbol?

(c)   Isabel .... El señor Méndez ....

¿Con quiénes van al teatro de vez en cuando?

(d)   Isabel .... El señor Méndez ....

¿A dónde salen, si no es al teatro?

(e)   Isabel .... Los señores Méndez ....

Documento número 13

Have a look at this advertisement. **Comparte tus fotos** means *share your photos* (note: it is **la foto**, being short for **la fotografía**). Now answer the questions below.

    (a) ¿Qué te ofrece este anuncio?

    (b) ¿Te gusta la foto aquí? (*Say, yes you do.*)

    (c) ¿Haces tú muchas fotos? (*Say, no you don't.*)

Para estudiar

Useful verbs

Here are some useful verbs which have already occurred here and there but which it would be helpful for you to learn in full. They belong in the groups mentioned in Unit 6 but you will see that some have slightly irregular forms. Learn the patterns of these verbs, which will help you with others later.

	dar *to give*	**ir** *to go*	**ver** *to see*
I	doy	voy	veo
you (tú)	das	vas	ves
he/she you (Vd.)	da	va	ve
we	damos	vamos	vemos
you (vosotros)	dais	vais	veis
they/you (Vds.)	dan	van	ven

	tener *to have*	**hacer** *to do, make*	**poner** *to put*
I	tengo	hago	pongo
you (tú)	tienes	haces	pones
he/she you (Vd.)	tiene	hace	pone
we	tenemos	hacemos	ponemos
you (vosotros)	tenéis	hacéis	ponéis
they/you (Vds.)	tienen	hacen	ponen

	decir *to say*	**seguir** *to follow*	**salir** *to leave, go out*
I	digo	sigo	salgo
you (tú)	dices	sigues	sales
he/she you (Vd.)	dice	sigue	sale

we	decimos	seguimos	salimos
you (vosotros)	decís	seguís	salís
they/you (Vds.)	dicen	siguen	salen

☑ ——————— Actividad ———————

2 To complete each sentence choose one of the various words
   or phrases given on the right.

(a) A Paco le gusta jugar …   (i)   toca
(b) Se va al gimnasio para …   (ii)   squash
(c) Generalmente, se juega al tenis en … (iii)   no le gusta
(d) Paco nada con sus amigos en …   (iv)   museos
(e) En invierno, Paco juega al …   (v)   verano
(f) Paco va siempre … para las   (vi)   a veces
vacaciones.   (vii)   ahora
(g) A Isabel … el deporte.   (viii) estar en forma
(h) Isabel … el piano y …   (ix)   partido
(i) Isabel sale … con sus amigos.   (x)   al teatro
(j) Isabel va a … y … cuando hay   (xi)   galerías
… especial.   (xii)   al tenis
(k) Señor Méndez no hace deporte …   (xiii) a Alicante
(l) Cuando hay un … de … en la   (xiv)   ponen
televisión, el señor Méndez   (xv)   la guitarra
… lo ve.   (xvi)   gustan
(m) Los señores Méndez van … a veces. (xvii)   fútbol
(n) En el Teatro de la Villa … las   (xviii) la piscina
zarzuelas. Les … a los señores   (xix)   siempre
Méndez las zarzuelas.   (xx)   una exposición

☐ ——————— Lectura ———————

Aquí tenemos entradas para dos centros patrocinados por el
Ayuntamiento de Madrid.

El Museo Municipal de Madrid es muy interesante: queda ilustra-
da toda la historia de la capital de España. Madrid tiene muchos
museos y galerías. El más importante es sin duda el Museo del
Prado, galería de arte de fama mundial.

El Teatro Español está especializado en la representación del teatro clásico de la literatura española. La entrada que tenemos aquí es para la función de la tarde, que empieza a las siete; hay otra función de la noche, que empieza a las diez o a las diez y media. Este teatro está subvencionado y las entradas no son muy caras.

patrocinado por	sponsored by
Ayuntamiento	Town Hall
sin duda	without doubt
mundial	world (adjective, the noun is **el mundo**)
empezar	start
subvencionado	subsidized
butaca	armchair, stalls (in the theatre)

Actividad

3 Look at the tickets and answer the questions:
   (a) ¿Dónde está el Museo Municipal de Madrid?
   (b) ¿Es necesario pagar para entrar en el museo?
   (c) ¿Qué número tiene la entrada?
   (d) ¿Para qué fecha es la entrada del teatro?
   (e) ¿Y para qué función?
   (f) ¿En qué fila está la butaca?

15

VIAJANDO POR ESPAÑA
Travelling in Spain

In this unit you will learn

- how to ask for and give directions
- how to talk about driving in Spain

Diálogos

Listen to, or read, the four short conversations below.

Aquí hay un plano (adaptado) de una parte de Madrid.

Diálogo 1

Isabel sale de la farmacia cuando una señora le pregunta:
Isabel is coming out of the chemist's when a lady asks her:

Señora	Perdone. ¿Puede Vd. decirme donde está Correos?
Isabel	Está allí. Al otro lado de la plaza.
Señora	Ya lo veo. Muchas gracias.

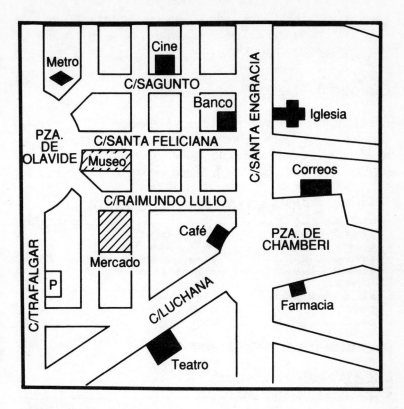

Diálogo 2

La señora Méndez sale del café cuando una chica le pregunta:
Señora Méndez is coming out of the café when a girl asks her:

Chica   Perdone, señora. ¿Hay una estación de Metro cerca de aquí?

Sra. Méndez   Sí. Toma la primera calle aquí a la izquierda, sigue hasta el final, y el metro está en el mismo lado de la plaza, a la derecha.

Diálogo 3

Paco está en la Plaza Olavide, cuando un señor le pregunta:

Señor   Oiga. ¿Hay un banco por aquí?

Paco   Sí. Tome esta calle – Santa Feliciana. Después de cruzar dos calles en la esquina de la tercera hay un banco, frente a la iglesia.

Diálogo 4

En el café, un chico pregunta al señor Méndez:

Chico   Perdone señor. ¿Cómo se va al cine Sagunto?

Sr. Méndez   Cuando sales de aquí, dobla a la izquierda, y toma la tercera calle también a la izquierda, después del banco. El cine está a la derecha.

Chico   Muchas gracias, señor.

puede Vd. decirme ...	could you tell me ...
Correos	the Post Office
ya lo veo	oh yes, I see it (lit. I've already seen it)
en el mismo lado	on the same side
al otro lado	on the other side
a la derecha/izquierda	to/on the right/left
tomar	to take
cruzar	cross
la esquina	corner
el tercero	the third (one)
frente a	opposite
la iglesia	church
doblar	to turn

Para estudiar

Telling people to do things

When the Méndez talk to the young people i.e. people they would address as **tú**, asking the way, they say **toma** (*take*). Paco, talking to an unknown older man, whom he would address as **Vd.**, says **tome** (*take*):

     toma (tú)   **tome (Vd.)**

When you are giving what amounts to a command, and you are talking to someone as **tú** the word will end with **-a** or **-e**, whichever is characteristic of the verb. For example:

toma	*take*
sigue	*follow, continue*
dobla	*turn*
pregunta	*ask*
bebe	*drink*
vuelve	*return*

However, if you are addressing someone as **Vd.,** the **–a** and **–e** are reversed. For example:

tome Vd.
siga Vd.
doble Vd.
pregunte Vd.
beba Vd.
vuelva Vd.

If this isn't confusing enough, there are several common forms of these commands which do not follow this pattern! These are best learnt as you meet them. For example, here are a few very useful ones:

di (tu)	*tell*	**dime (tu)**	*tell me*
diga (Vd.)	*tell*	**dígame (Vd.,)**	*tell me*
sal (tu)	*leave*	**salga (Vd)**	*leave*
¡Sal de aquí inmediatamente!		*Leave here immediately!*	

or, if you're desperate,

¡Fuera de aquí!   *Get right out of here!*

The whole business of the word forms to use when giving orders in Spanish, however, is fairly complicated; you may find it easier to learn them as you go rather than try to apply rules and then allow for exceptions. You can, of course avoid the whole problem by not throwing your weight about when in Spain, and making polite requests instead of issuing commands!

—————— Actividades ——————

1 Answer the questions with reference to the plan.
   (a) ¿Hay un parking (un aparcamiento) cerca del museo?
   (b) ¿Dónde está?

(c) ¿Qué hay frente a la iglesia?

(d) ¿En qué calle está el mercado?

(e) ¿Se puede ver la farmacia desde Correos?

(f) ¿El teatro y el café están en el mismo lado de la calle?

(g) ¿Cómo se va desde la plaza de Chamberí a la plaza de Olavide?

(h) La estación de metro ¿está más cerca del teatro o del cine?

(i) El banco de la calle Santa Engracia ¿en qué esquina está?

2 Now see if you can give directions to various people, using the map on page 123.

(a) You are standing in the calle Santa Engracia, just outside the church. A little girl asks you how to get to the Post Office. What do you say?

(b) You are leaving the cinema and an elderly gentleman asks you where the museum is. What do you say?

(c) As you emerge from the Metro station a lady asks you if there is a chemist's nearby. Direct her to the one in the Plaza de Chamberí.

(d) A teenager approaches you while you're sitting outside the café in Plaza de Chamberí, and asks you the way to the cinema. What do you say?

Lectura

Aquí hay un mapa de las carreteras principales de España.

Look at the map opposite and listen to or read the information about driving in Spain. Refer to the vocabulary if necessary, but see how much you can understand. If you have the cassette, listen to it in whole paragraphs, repeating as necessary, rather than using the pause button.

Uno modo muy conveniente de viajar por España para conocer sus viejas ciudades y su paisaje es ir en coche. Pero hay que tener en cuenta que España es un país de lejanos horizontes: las distancias pueden ser grandes. Además, en verano puede hacer un calor intenso y muchas horas en coche pueden resultar insoportables. Sin embargo, si se planea un itinerario práctico y si se escoge una

época del año apropiada, es agradable viajar por las buenas carreteras que ofrece España al turista.

Como vemos en el pequeño mapa, muchas carreteras principales radian de Madrid. La que va al norte es la Nacional I, que llega a San Sebastián y la frontera francesa, pasando por Burgos. La carretera de Cataluña, la Nacional II, va desde Madrid a Barcelona. Es la Nacional III que va a Valencia, y la IV es la carretera de Andalucía. La carretera de Portugal, la Nacional V, cruza la frontera cerca de Badajoz; la carretera de Galicia termina en La Coruña y es la Nacional VI.

España tiene también muchos kilómetros de autopistas, que son casi todas de peaje. Las más importantes son tal vez la autopista que va por la costa desde Francia hasta más allá de Alicante, y la que conecta Bilbao y Barcelona, grandes centros industriales.

Como siempre, hay que conducir con precaución, y no ir demasiado rápido. En España hay un elevado porcentaje de accidentes. Sobre todo hay que evitar las fechas en julio y agosto cuando millones de españoles se desplazan para sus vacaciones.

el paisaje	landscape
tener en cuenta	bear in mind
un país	a country
lejano	distant
además	besides, moreover
el calor	heat
resultar	to turn out to be, prove to be
insoportable	unbearable
sin embargo	nevertheless, however
si se planea	if you plan
escoger	to choose
época	time, period
agradable	pleasant, agreeable
la carretera	road
radiar	to radiate
el norte	the north
la frontera	frontier
desde ... hasta	from ... to, until
terminar	to end
la autopista	motorway
de peaje	toll-paying
tal vez	perhaps
más allá	beyond
conducir	drive
un elevado porcentaje	a high percentage, a high rate
desplazarse	to move from one place to another

 ——————— **Actividades** ———————

3 Answer the following questions, with reference to the passage and the map above.

(a) Para ir desde Madrid a Cádiz, ¿qué carretera hay que tomar? ¿Se pasa por Granada?

(b) ¿Dónde se cruza la frontera, si se va desde Madrid a Portugal?

(c) ¿Hay mucha distancia entre Gijón y Oviedo?

(d) ¿Madrid está cerca de Toledo?

(e) ¿Cuál está más cerca de Madrid, Valencia o Barcelona?

(f) Para ir desde Francia a Alicante, ¿qué carretera se toma?

(g) ¿Qué ciudades hay entre Badajoz y Gijón?

(h) ¿Cuál es más grande, España o Portugal?

(i) ¿Santiago está en Galicia o en Cataluña?

4 You have just come home from a driving holiday in Spain, and your Argentinian friend, Pedro, is asking you about it. Fill in the blanks according to the guidelines to complete your conversation.

Pedro   Dime, ¿hay buenas carreteras en España?

(a) *You*   *Say yes, the roads are good, but the distances are great.*

Pedro   ¿Viajar en coche, es un modo bueno de ver el paisaje?

(b) *You*   *Say yes, and you like the distant horizons.*

Pedro   ¿Hace mucho calor en mayo en España?

(c) *You*   *Say it is hot in May, but in July, August and September it is intensely hot, and it is unbearable to spend the whole day in the car.*

Pedro   ¿Hay autopistas en España?

(d) *You*   *Say, yes, but they are toll-charging, and you prefer the smaller roads. Nevertheless, you like the motorway that connects Bilbao and Barcelona.*

Pedro   ¿Hay demasiados coches en las carreteras?

(e) *You*   *Say not in May, but you still have to drive carefully and not go too fast. In July and August, there are too many cars because millions of Spanish families are going from one place to another for their holidays.*

16

——NO ME SIENTO BIEN——
I feel unwell

In this unit you will learn

● useful vocabulary for dealing with minor health problems

 —————— **Para estudiar** ——————

Saying where it hurts and that you feel ill

If you're unlucky enough to fall ill while in a Spanish-speaking country, you'll need to know how to say what the problem is. Here is the basic way of indicating where a pain is. We use **me duele/me duelen** (literally *it hurts me/they hurt me*) with the name(s) of the part(s) affected. It works in the same way as the use of **me gusta/me gustan**, or **me apetece** that we learned in unit 9. For example, you say:

Me duele **la cabeza.**   Me duele **una muela.**

to say that you have a headache or toothache. Here are some other parts of the body which can hurt:

Me duele el cuello.	*neck*
Me duele el estómago.	*stomach*
Me duele la espalda.	*back*

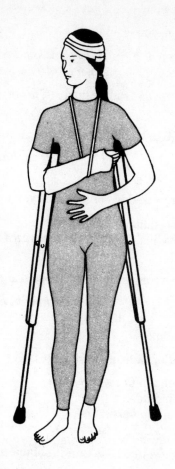

Me duele el brazo.	*arm*
Me duele la mano.	*hand*
Me duele la pierna.	*leg*
Me duele el pie.	*foot*

Note we say **la mano**: even though the word ends in **-o**.
If the pain you feel is the result of a blow or knock, you can say:

Me he dado un golpe en la cabeza.	*I have hit my head.*

(This literally means *I have given myself a blow on the head*.) Or:

Me he dado un golpe en el pie.   *I have knocked my foot.*

Speaking of a third person, you would say

Se ha dado un golpe en la   *He/she has knocked his/*
   cabeza/el pie.   *her head/foot.*

Notice you say *the head*, *the foot* rather than *my*, *his* or *her head* or *foot*, etc..

If you are unlucky enough to be bitten or stung you would say:

Tengo una picadura   *I have stung my hand.*
   en la mano

Of a child who has cut or grazed his or her knee you would say:

Tiene un corte en la rodilla.   *He/she has cut his/her knee.*
or Se ha rasguñado la rodilla.   *He/she has grazed his/her*
                               knee.

Other things that can go wrong on holiday in Spain are:

Tengo algo en el ojo.   *I've something in my eye.*
Tengo el ojo irritado.
Tengo el ojo inflamado.

(Words like **irritado, inflamado** are easily guessed.)

Tengo el tobillo hinchado (*a swollen ankle*).
Tengo la piel (*skin*) irritada.
Tengo una quemadura (*a burn*).
Tengo una quemadura del sol (*sunburn*).

(Sunstroke – rather more serious – is **una insolación**.)

Tengo diarrea.
Tengo colitis.

These last two are obvious. They are easily avoidable if you wash or peel all fruit, wash salads very thoroughly, and drink only from hygienic sources (and refuse ice in drinks unless you are sure of it).

Tengo fiebre.   *I have a temperature.*
Se toma la temperatura con   *You take a temperature*
   un termómetro.   *with a thermometer.*
La temperatura normal es de   *A normal temperature is*
   treinta y siete grados (37°).   *37°C.*

El niño tiene unas décimas.   *The boy has a slight temperature.* (**unas décimas**, *a few tenths of a degree.*)

We have already had **estoy constipado** (see Unit 4). You can also say:

Tengo un catarro.

Now for some remedies. For minor emergencies a visit to the chemist will probably suffice, and if you can explain the problem he or she will be able to provide an appropriate remedy. We hope you will not need to ask for:

un médico (*a doctor*)
un dentista
las horas de consulta (*surgery hours*)
una clínica
un hospital

--- **Actividad** ---

1 Your friend Ignacio is a hypochondriac. You make the mistake of asking him how he is. Complete your own part of the conversation (use **tú**).

(a) *You*   *Say hello and ask him how he is.*
Ignacio   No estoy muy bien. No sé lo que me pasa. Me duele todo.
(b) *You*   *Ask him if he has a cold.*
Ignacio   No. Pero no me siento bien.
(c) *You*   *Ask him if he has a temperature.*
Ignacio   No sé. Voy a poner el termómetro. ¿Qué dice?
(d) *You*   *Tell him it says 37°. He hasn't got a temperature.*
Ignacio   Estoy seguro que tengo una insolación.
(e) *You*   *Ask him if he has a headache.*
Ignacio   Sí. Me duele mucho.
(f) *You*   *And a stomach ache?*
Ignacio   Sí. Me duele un poco.
(g) *You*   *Tell him he doesn't feel well because he drinks too much.*

Documento número 14

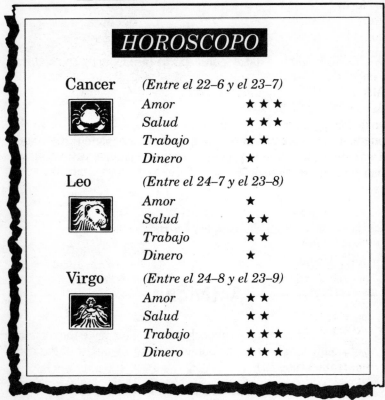

HOROSCOPO

Cancer *(Entre el 22–6 y el 23–7)*

Amor	★ ★ ★
Salud	★ ★ ★
Trabajo	★ ★
Dinero	★

Leo *(Entre el 24–7 y el 23–8)*

Amor	★
Salud	★ ★
Trabajo	★ ★
Dinero	★

Virgo *(Entre el 24–8 y el 23–9)*

Amor	★ ★
Salud	★ ★
Trabajo	★ ★ ★
Dinero	★ ★ ★

Aquí hay un horóscopo para tres meses del verano. ¿Cuál es el signo más afortunado, Cancer, Leo o Virgo?

 ———————— **Lectura** ————————

———————— **La farmacia** ————————

El señor o la señora que trabaja en la farmacia es el *farmacéutico* o la *farmacéutica*. La farmacia se indica con una cruz verde. En general, se puede comprar medicamentos en la farmacia sin receta médica. Un medicamento puede ser un antibiótico, un antiséptico, o un analgésico, y puede tener la forma de unas píldoras o unos comprimidos, una pomada, una loción, una medicina, o unas gotas.

Penicilina es un antibiótico. Alcohol es un antiséptico. Aspirina y codeína son analgésicos. Para una alergia se puede tomar unas píldoras antihistaminas, o poner una inyección. También en la farmacia se puede comprar una venda, unas tiritas, una tobillera, o algodón en rama, preservativos, y muchas otras cosas.

una cruz verde	a green cross
comprar	to buy
sin receta médica	without a medical prescription
píldoras, comprimidos	pills, tablets
una pomada	cream
gotas	drops
una alergia	allergy
una venda	bandage
tiritas	sticking plasters
una tobillera	ankle support
algodón en rama	cotton wool
preservativos	contraceptives

Actividad

2 You have all kinds of minor problems and go to the chemist's for some help. Can you make the following requests?
(a) Ask if they have a lotion for sunburn.
(b) Say that you have cut your foot and ask for an antiseptic cream and a bandage.
(c) Say that you have a stomach ache.
(d) Say that you have toothache and ask for a painkiller.

(e) Say that your son does not feel well and that he has a tem
perature.

(f) Ask for drops for an inflamed eye.

(g) Say that your ankle is swollen and you want an elastic sup
port.

(h) Say that you need to see a doctor and ask what his
surgery hours are.

 —————————— **Lectura** ——————————

Finally in this unit, let us look at a sample of Spanish which makes
no concessions at all for the learner. Let us suppose that someone
in your family has an inflammation of the throat, and the chemist
provides you with a throat spray, which he recommends for all
types of mouth and throat infections. Here is the leaflet you find
inside the package. How much of it can you understand?

Anginovag®

Composición

Por 100 ml.:

Dequalinium cloruro (D.C.I.)	0,100 g.
Enoxolona (D.C.I.)	0,060 g.
Acetato de hidrocortisona (D.C.I.)	0,060 g.
Tirotricina (D.C.I.)	0,400 g.
Lidocaína clorhidrato (D.C.I.)	0,100 g.
Sacarina sódica	0,320 g.
Excipiente aromatizado c.s.p.	70,000 ml.
Propelente (Diclorodifluormetano)	c.s.

Indicaciones

Tratamiento preventivo-curativo de las afecciones bucofaringeas:
Amigdalitis. Faringitis. Laringitis. Estomatitis. Ulceras y Aftas bucales. Glositis.

Dosificación

Dosis de ataque: 1–2 aplicaciones cada 2–3 horas.
Dosis de sostén o como preventivo: 1 aplicación cada 6 horas.

Normas para la correcta aplicación del preparado

Abrir bien la boca. Dirigir la boquilla inhaladora hacia la región afectada (garganta, boca, lengua, etc … según casos).
Presionar la parte superior de la cápsula de arriba a abajo hasta el tope, manteniendo el frasco en posición vertical.
El frasco se halla provisto de una válvula dosificadora: cada presión hasta el tope origina la salida regulada de medicamento.

Contraindicaciones, efectos secundarios e incompatibilidades

No se conocen.

Intoxicación y posible tratamiento

Dada la escasa toxicidad del preparado, no se prevé la intoxicación, ni aún accidental.

Presentación

Envases conteniendo 20 ml.

Los medicamentos deben mantenerse fuera del alcance de los niños.

LABORATORIOS NOVAG, S.A.
Director Técnico: X. Vila Coca
Buscallá s/n – San Cugat del Vallés
Barcelona – España

Comentario

There will be much of this that is incomprehensible, but you should be able to decipher the most important parts, which say what the preparation is for, and give the dosage. The second section, **Indicaciones**, says that this product is suitable for, amongst other things, tonsillitis (**amígdalas** *tonsils*), pharingitis, laryngitis and mouth ulcers. The dosage for treatment is one or two applications every two or three hours, or one every six hours as a preventative. (**cada** is a useful word, meaning *each* or *every*.) Further down, you can probably work out that there seem to be no possible side effects or harmful results from over-dosage. The middle section is the most difficult to unravel – it tells you how to use the spray. **Una válvula dosificadora** is a valve which regulates the amount released with each downwards pressure of the button. The last line is the usual warning that medicines should be kept out of the reach of children.

—————— Actividad ——————

3 Answer these questions based on the information in the leaflet.
   (a) ¿Cómo se llama el medicamento?
   (b) El medicamento ¿es un spray o es una medicina?
   (c) ¿Cuántos mililitros tiene el envase?
   (d) ¿Para qué clase de infección es el tratamiento?
   (e) ¿Cuál es la dosis preventiva?
   (f) ¿Y la dosis curativa?
   (g) ¿Hay efectos secundarios?
   (h) ¿Dónde se fabrica el medicamento?

Check with the key if you find these questions difficult and then study the leaflet again to see how the Spanish works.

17

VAMOS DE COMPRAS
Let's go shopping

In this unit you will learn

- about shopping in the market
- about shopping in a department store

Preámbulo

The advent of the supermarket and the hypermarket has made some shopping a non-language experience in that it is possible to buy most common items without speaking a word of Spanish. However, 'real' shopping, where you need to make your wants known to the shopkeeper, can be great fun. Much everyday shopping in Spain takes place at the stall of a covered market. This is the aspect we shall tackle first in this unit.

Lectura

La señora Méndez va de compras con su marido. En la frutería-verdulería compra:

2 kg. de naranjas	(*oranges*)
$\frac{1}{2}$ kg. de limones	(*lemons*)

1 kg. de peras	(*pears*)
½ kg. de fresas	(*strawberries*)
1 kg. de patatas	(*potatoes*)
½ kg. de acelgas	(*Swiss chard*)
una lechuga	(*a lettuce*)
½ kg. de tomates	(*tomatoes*)
dos ajos	(*two heads of garlic*)

En la pescadería hay:

salmón	
truchas	(*trout*)
pescadilla	(*whiting*)
bonito	
gambas	(*prawns*)
sardinas	

pero por fin compra dos rajas de merluza (*two pieces of hake*).
En la carnicería compra:

dos filetes de ternera	(*two fillets of veal*)
½ kg. de carne picada	(*minced meat*)

Ahora el pobre señor Méndez tiene cuatro bolsas y no puede llevar más. Pero está obligado a esperar mientras su mujer va a la
droguería-perfumería a comprar detergente, lejía, jabón y colonia.
Después se van despacio a casa, pasando por la panadería, donde
la señora compra pan y también leche.

▣ Comentario

You can see what Sra. Méndez buys and deduce which shops or
market stalls she goes to. At the end Sr. Méndez is laden with four
bags and can't carry any more. But he still has to wait while his
wife goes to buy detergent, bleach, soap and eau de cologne. Then
they go slowly home, calling at the baker's where she buys bread
and milk.

✷ Note that a **droguería** sells household goods for cleaning; a
droguería-perfumería will sell toiletries as well. Señora Méndez
does not on this occasion buy ham – **el jamón** – or cooked meats
which she would get in **una charcutería**. A stall or shop which

sells cheese – **el queso** – is **una quesería**, and eggs – **los huevos** – can be brought at **una huevería**. A general grocery store is called **una tienda de comestibles** or (more old-fashioned) **una tienda de ultramarinos**.

Actividad

---

1   Let us return to Sra. Méndez and her shopping. This is what the **frutero** says as he tots up her bill. Read it aloud, putting all the figures into words, and look at his scribbled addition.

NARANJAS	150
LIMONES	45
PERAS	100
FRESAS	120
PATATAS	80
ACELGAS	65
LECHUGA	95
TOMATES	60
AJOS	40
	755

'¿Nada más, senora? Pues son dos kilos de naranjas, a 75 el kilo, 150 pesetas; cuarto de limones, 45 pesetas; un kilo de peras, 100 pesetas; medio de fresas, 120; patatas 80, medio de acelgas, 65 pesetas; la lechuga, 95; y los tomates 60; ajos 40. Vamos a ver – 5, 10, 15. Llevamos 1; 4 y 1, 5; y 6, 11; y 9, 20; y 6, 26; y 8, 34; y 2, 36; y 4, 40; y 5, 45. Llevamos 4. 5, 6 y 7. 755 pesetas en total, señora.'

Notice **Llevamos 1, llevamos 4** – *carry 1, carry 4*.
La Sra. Méndez le da 800 ptas. El frutero dice '¿Tiene Vd. un duro? Gracias. Así que le doy diez duros de cambio.'

Comentario

Diez duros de cambio   *Fifty pesetas change*

Un duro is five pesetas – a very common expression. The greengrocer asks Señor Méndez if she has the odd five pesetas so that he can give her **diez duros**, i.e. fifty pesetas, change. One hundred pesetas is often referred to as **veinte duros**, ten pesetas are **dos duros**, etc.

☑ Documento número 15

Four packets of biscuits for the price of three!

Look carefully at the advert and then answer these questions:
(a) ¿De que están rellenadas las galletas?
(b) ¿Cuánto pesa un paquete?
(c) ¿Dónde se recomienda almacenar las galletas?

 ——————— **Para estudiar** ———————

Here is a list of common shops and shopkeepers and what they sell.

En la pescadería	el pescadero	vende pescado.
En la carnicería	el carnicero	vende carne (la carne).
En la panadería	el panadero	vende pan (el pan).
En la pastelería	el pastelero	vende pasteles (los pasteles, *cakes*).
En la lechería	el lechero	vende leche (la leche).
En la librería	el librero	vende libros.
En la farmacia	el farmacéutico	vende medicamentos.
En la frutería-verdulería	el frutero	vende fruta y verduras.
En la droguería	se vende	artículos de limpieza

En un quiosco   se vende   periódicos y revistas
¡En un supermercado se vende de todo!
Un librería is *not* a library, it's a bookshop. A library is **una biblioteca.**

Lectura

Large department stores are referred to as **grandes almacenes**.

En un gran almacén hay muchos departmentos y se vende muchísimas cosas – muebles, cristalería, ropa, etc, etc. En España el más famoso es tal vez 'El Corte Inglés' que tiene sucursales en Madrid y en otras ciudades de España. Cuando se compra algo en un gran almacén se puede pagar con dinero o con tarjeta de crédito (Visa, Access, etc). El dependiente pregunta '¿En efectivo?' para saber cómo se va a pagar. Cuando se paga con tarjeta de crédito hay que tener otro documento (por ejemplo un pasaporte) para comprobar su identidad. Es muy conveniente pagar con tarjeta porque así se evita el riesgo de llevar mucho dinero en la cartera. Por lo general se recibe la cuenta de Visa o de Access al mes siguiente en su domicilio. Claro, no se puede pagar con tarjeta en la frutería o la carnicería, etc.

los muebles	furniture	**la identidad**	identity
la cristalería	glassware	**evitar**	to avoid
la ropa	clothing	**el riesgo**	risk
el sucursal	branch, outlet	**el dinero**	money
en efectivo	in cash	**la cartera**	wallet, purse
comprobar	to prove	**recibir**	to receive
la cuenta	the bill	**siguiente**	following
claro	obviously		

Actividades

2   Shopping practice. Ask for:
   (a) 2 kilos of oranges.
   (b) 200 grammes of ham.
   (c) a litre of milk.

    (d) 150 grammes of cheese.
    (e) 2 heads of garlic.
    (f) a kilo of potatoes.
    (g) 250 grammes (**un cuarto** – $\frac{1}{4}$ kg.) of prawns.
    (h) 3 salmon steaks.

3 You are in a department store.
    (a) Ask where the perfumery department is.
    (b) Ask if there is a pharmacy.
    (c) Ask where the cafeteria is.
    (d) Say you would like to pay by Visa.
    (e) Say you will pay cash.
    (f) Ask what floor the sports department is on.
    (g) Ask where the cloakrooms are.
    (h) Say that the bookshop is on the ground floor.

18

COMIENDO Y BEBIENDO
Eating and drinking

In this unit you will learn

- how to order in a bar, café or restaurant
- a little about Spanish cooking and the dishes and drinks available

---
Diálogo

Pizzas – servicio a domicilio *Take-away pizzas*

Isabel pasa la tarde en casa de Paco. Van a ir al teatro.

Paco	Tengo hambre. ¿Quieres comer algo antes de ir al teatro?
Isabel	Pues yo también tengo hambre. ¿Qué tienes en casa para comer?
Paco	Poca cosa, creo. ¿Llamamos para una pizza? Aquí tengo la lista. ¿Qué pizza quieres?
Isabel	A mí me gustan las pizzas de queso. ¿Pedimos una de cuatro quesos, que está aquí en la lista? ¿Te apetece?
Paco	Vale. Voy a llamar al centro más cercano.

PIZZAS	Pizza Completa
• PIZZA DE AHUMADOS: (tomate, Mozzarella, salmón, anchoas) • PIZZA DE CARNE: (tomate, Mozzarella, carne) • PIZZA CUATRO QUESOS: (tomate, Mozzarella, manchego, parmesano, roquefort) • SUPER RING RING: (tomate, Mozzarella, gambas, jamón serrano, champiñón, pimiento morrón)	1.325

SU PROPIA PIZZA	Pizza Base
• PIZZA DE QUESO Y TOMATE: Sobre la base de nuestra pizza de queso y tomate usted puede añadir cualquiera de los siguientes ingredientes:	1.100

		Cada Ingrediente
• DOBLE QUESO • JAMON YORK • SALAMI • CHORIZO • PIMIENTO MORRON	• ANCHOAS • ACEITUNAS • CEBOLLA • CHAMPIÑON • BACON	125

BEBIDAS	Unidad
• COCA COLA • FANTA LIMON • FANTA NARANJA • CERVEZA	125

Llame al Centro más cercano.

Guzmán el Bueno
(Esq. Joaquín María López)
• 544 60 80
• 544 79 72

MAJADAHONDA
Doctor Calero, 32 - Bis
• 638 63 13
• 638 64 00

Serrano, 41
• 577 29 79
• 577 38 31
• 577 38 32

Beba
Coca-Cola
MARCA REG.

Zonas de reparto limitadas.

Alberto Alcocer
• 259 94 00
• 259 99 09

Torre Picasso

Centro Comercial
Arturo Soria Plaza

Proximamente:
Av. Bruselas, 72

Centro Comercial
Parque Sur

---

más cercano	nearest
¿pedimos?	shall we ask for?
servicio a domicilio	home delivery service
anchoas	anchovies
manchego . . .	an excellent Spanish . . .
(queso manchego)	cheese from La Mancha region
gambas	prawns
jamón	ham (two sorts – serrano and York)
champiñón	mushroom
pimiento morrón	red pepper (sweet pepper, usually in brine)
aceitunas	olives
cebolla	onion

Actividad

1. (a) Say that you are hungry.
   (b) Ask what there is to eat.
   (c) Ask someone else if he/she is hungry.
   (d) Say you like pizzas.
   (e) Ask someone else if he/she would like a pizza.
   (f) Ask if he/she would like an anchovy pizza or a ham pizza.
   (g) Say you'll ring for a pizza.
   (h) Ask your friend if he/she wants beer or a coke.
   (i) Say you'll buy two beers.
   (j) Say you're going to have a coffee.

Diálogo

Los señores Méndez van al café   *The señores Méndez go to the café*

Los Méndez entran en una cafetería. Van a merendar.

Camarero	Buenas tardes, señores. ¿Qué van a tomar?
Sr. Méndez	Para mí un café con leche.
Camarero	¿Y para Vd., señora?
Sra. Méndez	Para mí un té con limón. ¿Qué tiene de pastelería?
Camarero	Hay tarta de manzana, pastel de chocolate, tostada …
Sra. Méndez	Una ración de pastel, por favor.
Sr. Méndez	Voy a tomar una tostada.
Camarero	¿La quiere con miel, o con mermelada?
Sr. Méndez	Solo con mantequilla.
Camarero	Muy bien, señores, en seguida.

merendar	to have afternoon 'tea'
miel	honey
mermelada	jam (not just marmalade)
mantequilla	butter
manzana	apple
tostada	toast

Actividades

2 The statements below refer to the two dialogues. Choose one of the phrases from the right to complete each of the sentences on the left.

(a) A Isabel le gustan muchísimo
- (i) las gambas.
- (ii) las anchoas.
- (iii) los quesos.

(b) Paco tiene hambre pero
- (i) no le gusta comer en casa.
- (ii) tiene poco a comer en casa.
- (iii) prefiere beber.

(c) Después de comer su pizza, Paco y Isabel
- (i) llaman por teléfono.
- (ii) van al teatro.
- (iii) van a la pizzería.

(d) Hoy los señores Méndez van a la cafetería para
- (i) tomar un chocolate.
- (ii) merendar.
- (iii) hablar con el camarero.

(e) La señora Méndez pregunta al camarero
- (i) qué hay de pastelería.
- (ii) si tiene un té con limón.
- (iii) qué quiere su marido.

(f) El señor Méndez toma
- (i) una ración de pastel.
- (ii) una tostada con queso.
- (iii) una tostada con mantequilla.

3 Ask a friend (**tú**) if he/she wants:
- (a) a coffee
- (b) tea with lemon
- (c) chocolate tart
- (d) toast with honey
- (e) a cold beer.

Now put the same questions to an acquaintance (**Vd.**)

———————— Lectura ————————

Donde comer y beber   *Where to eat and drink*

En España, hay muchos restaurantes y muchísimos bares en todas partes. Y también hay la combinación de las dos cosas – el bar-restaurante. En un bar-restaurante se puede desayunar, comer, cenar, tomar el aperitivo, tomar un café, o merendar. Los españoles en general no desayunan mucho – toman un café con leche y pan. Por eso a mediodía muchos de ellos tienen hambre y van a un bar a tomar una cerveza y tapas. *Tapas* son pequeñas porciones de comida y hay una gran variedad: mariscos, pescado, carne, tortilla, queso, chorizo y salchichón, etcétera, etcétera. Comer en pequeñas porciones se llama *picar.*

Comentario

The above passage says that there are many restaurants and very many bars everywhere in Spain. The two are also combined in the bar-restaurant, where one can breakfast, have lunch or dinner, have supper, have afternoon 'tea', or an aperitif or a coffee. In general Spaniards don't have much breakfast, just milky coffee with bread, and so many of them are hungry at midday and go to a bar for a beer and **tapas**. There is a great variety of tapas – seafood, fish, meat, omelette, cheese, Spanish sausages. The word **picar** is used to denote eating these snacks with a drink. (lit. *to peck*!)

The verb **comer** means *to eat*, in general; it also means to have the main meal of the day. Thus the word **comida** can mean food in general, a meal, or the main, early afternoon meal. The verb **merendar** means *to have a snack*, usually coffee, tea, cake or similar, in the later afternoon. It can also mean *a picnic*, of any kind. The name of the meal is **la merienda**, e.g. *Let's take a picnic*, **Vamos a llevar una merienda**.

Documento número 16

Here is some information about a cafe in the Calle Sagunto (see Unit 15). It is decorated in the style of the beginning of the 20th century, and specialises in rice dishes (**arroces**) and champagne-style wines (**cavas**).

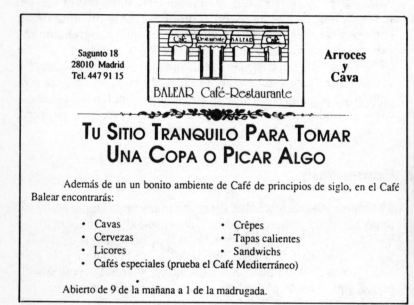

Sagunto 18
28010 Madrid
Tel. 447 91 15

BALEAR Café-Restaurante

Arroces
y
Cava

TU SITIO TRANQUILO PARA TOMAR UNA COPA O PICAR ALGO

Además de un un bonito ambiente de Café de principios de siglo, en el Café Balear encontrarás:

- Cavas
- Cervezas
- Licores
- Cafés especiales (prueba el Café Mediterráneo)

- Crêpes
- Tapas calientes
- Sandwichs

Abierto de 9 de la mañana a 1 de la madrugada.

(a) What else do they serve?
(b) When is it open?

──────────── Lectura ────────────

Platos y vinos de España

La cocina española es muy variada. Todas las regiones de España tienen sus platos típicos, por ejemplo la *paella*, que es de la región de Valencia. Se ofrece la paella a los turistas en todas partes, pero es un plato valenciano, porque allí se cultiva el arroz. Es evidente que es el clima y la agricultura de la región que determinan como son los platos regionales. En el norte, se come *fabada* en Asturias, *mariscos* en Galicia (que tiene mucha costa y barcos de pescar), y *bacalao* en Bilbao. Se come *cocido* en Castilla, y muchos *fritos* en Andalucía, donde se produce muchísimo aceite de oliva. También de Andalucía es la famosa sopa fría *gazpacho*, preparado a base de aceite y tomate. España produce muchos vinos. Las cuatro regiones principales son:

Jérez de la Frontera

El vino de Jérez tiene fama mundial como aperitivo. Se exporta mucho a Inglaterra. También en Jérez se produce el coñac.

Valdepeñas

Al sur de Madrid, produce vinos tintos que se maduran en enormes *tinajas*.

La Rioja

Los grandes vinos de La Rioja son de los mejores que hay. Tienen un sabor único que se deriva de su maduración en barriles de roble.

Cataluña

En el Penedés de Cataluña se produce buenos vinos blancos.

la cocina	kitchen, or cuisine
el arroz	rice
la fabada	bean stew, with black pudding and fat bacon
el bacalao	cod, dried first and then soaked and cooked
el cocido	stew of meats with chick peas (**garbanzos**), served with green vegetables as equivalent to three courses – soup, vegetables and meat
fritos	fried dishes
el aceite	oil
se maduran	they mature
tinaja	huge earthenware jar
un sabor único	a unique flavour
barriles de roble	oak barrels

En el restaurante

Aquí está el menú. ¿Qué va a tomar?

RESTAURANTE LA GOLONDRINA
Menú del día

Sopa de verduras
Entremeses
Tortilla a la española
Judías verdes
****

Merluza a la romana
Filete de ternera
Pollo al ajillo
con
Ensalada mixta
Patatas fritas
****

Flan
Helado de vainilla o chocolate
Fruta
****

Precio 900 ptas.
Pan y vino/agua mineral incluido

Comentario

For the first course you have a choice between vegetable soup, hors d'oeuvres, Spanish omelette and green beans. The main course offers fried hake, fillet of veal or chicken cooked with finely chopped garlic, all served with a mixed salad and chipped potatoes. For dessert (**postre**) there is caramel custard (not a fruit tart!), vanilla or chocolate ice-cream or fruit. Bread and wine or mineral water are included in the price.

Actividad

4 Fill in the blanks to complete your conversation with the waiter.

Camarero   Buenos días. ¿Qué va a tomar? ¿De primer plato?

(a) *You*	*Say you'd like the green beans.*
Camarero	¿Y segundo plato?
(b) *You*	*Say you like chicken, but not garlic, You'll take the hake.*
Camarero	¿Y de postre?
(c) *You*	*Say you want ice cream for dessert.*
Camarero	¿Prefiere helado de vanilla o de chocolate?
(d) *You*	*You prefer chocolate.*
Camarero	Agua mineral con gas o sin gas?
(e) *You*	*Say still, please.*
Camarero	¿Quiere vino blanco o tinto?
(f) *You*	*With the fish, perhaps white.*
Camarero	¿Va a tomar café? ¿Café con leche o café solo?
(g) *You*	*Say you don't want coffee, if it's not included.*

5 There are some other details you'd like to know. Ask the waiter:
   (a) What the hors d'oeuvres are.
   (b) Whether the hake is fresh (**fresca**).
   (c) If the chicken has a lot of garlic.
   (d) What fruit there is.
   (e) If the wine comes from La Rioja.
   (f) Whether you can have beer instead of wine.

19

ASUNTOS PRÁCTICOS
Some practical matters

In this unit you will learn

- how to use the telephone
- how to change money at the bank
- how to buy stamps and post letters
- what to do in emergencies

Lectura

El cambio

Los turistas que visitan España tienen que ir al banco muchas veces para cambiar dinero. Aunque se puede cambiar dinero en hoteles y otros centros comerciales, en general el cambio no es tan favorable como en los bancos. En el banco hay que buscar la ventanilla donde dice 'Cambio'. Se puede cambiar billetes – libras, dólares, marcos, francos – o cheques de viaje. También se puede sacar dinero con una tarjeta de banco. El turista necesita mostrar su pasaporte para comprobar su identidad. Después de comprobar la documentación hay que ir a la caja donde el cajero entrega el dinero.

El horario de los bancos es de lunes a viernes desde las 0830 hasta las 1400 horas. Los sábados sólo están abiertos desde las 0830 hasta las 1230 horas. Los domingos y días de fiesta están cerrados. En verano tienen un horario modificado y están cerrados los sábados.

Comentario

Tourists visiting Spain often have to go to the bank to change money. Although one can change money in hotels and other commercial establishments, the rate is not usually as favourable as in the banks. In the bank you have to look for the window where it says 'Exchange'. One can change notes – pounds, dollars, marks, francs – or travellers' cheques. The tourist has to show his passport to prove his identity. After checking the documentation one has to go to the cash-desk where the cashier hands over the money.

Check the above translation with the Spanish version and note the meanings of the new words. The second paragraph should be clear – it gives the usual opening times of banks in Spain. Particularly useful is:

hay que	*one must*

and the phrase:

los turistas tienen que	*the tourists have to*

Other examples of the use of this sort of word group are:

Tengo que	*I have to*
Tengo que ir	*I have to go*
Paco tiene que comprar ...	*Paco has to buy ...*
Tenemos que visitar ...	*We have to visit ...*

Correos

Para mandar cartas y postales hay que comprar sellos. Los sellos se venden en Correos y también en estancos. Un estanco es una tienda pequeña donde se vende tabaco, cerillas, postales y, claro, sellos para la correspondencia. Las cartas a otros países se mandan por avión. Se puede pedir 'un sello para Inglaterra/para los Estados Unidos/para Australia, etc. por favor'. Se echa la carta en un buzón. El buzón está pintado de amarillo.

mandar	to send
la carta	letter
la postal	postcard
el sello	postage stamp
el estanco	tobacconist's
las cerillas	matches
pedir	to ask for, request
echar	to post (lit..to throw)
el buzón	postbox
pintado	painted
amarillo	yellow

Necesidades personales

Para ir al W.C. en una ciudad en España generalmente hay que entrar en un café o en un bar. Se pregunta 'Por favor, ¿los servicios?' o en un hotel más elegante '¿Los aseos, por favor?'. En las puertas dice *Caballeros* o *Señoras*.

| servicos | conveniences |
| los aseos | cloakroom ,washroom (a cloak room where one leaves coats is **un guardarropas**) |

Actividad

1 Work through the following exercise, based on the above three study sections. Check with the key if there are any words you don't know, or have forgotten.

How would you, in Spanish:

(a) ask if you can change money in the hotel?

(b) say that you want to change one hundred pounds sterling?

(c) ask what the rate of exchange is?

(d) say that you prefer to go to a bank?

(e) ask what time the bank closes?
(f) say that you must get to the bank before two o'clock?
(g) say that you have travellers' cheques in dollars?
(h) ask where the cash desk is?
(i) ask where you can buy stamps?
(j) say that you want two stamps for airmail letters to the United States and five stamps for postcards to England?
(k) say that you have to post the letters today?
(l) ask where the nearest letter-box is?
(m) ask where the cloakroom is? (either sort)

Repeat the exercise with progressively less checking with the **Clave** until you are fluent.

Documento número 17

When this notice appeared, the *Banco Atlántico* was offering a rate of 11.75% on a special deposit account for sums between 5 and 24 million pesetas.

T.A.E. is the equivalent to English C.A.R. – compound annual rate. What do you think **Sin comisiones** and **Sin retención fiscal** mean?

Lectura

Como llamar por teléfono

A veces se necesita llamar por teléfono a casa. Se puede hacer llamadas internacionales desde un teléfono público o desde el teléfono de un hotel. También se puede hacer llamadas de 'cobro revertido'. Para una llamada internacional hay que marcar el numero 07 y esperar el tono. Después se marca el prefijo del país (Inglaterra es 44, los Estados Unidos es 1, Francia es 33), la ciudad (para Inglaterra sin el cero, por ejemplo Londres es 71 no 071, Los Angeles es 213) seguido del número del abonado. Si se oye un tono interrumpido rápido significa que está comunicando.

la llamada	call
una llamada de cobro revertido	a reverse charge call
marcar	to dial
el prefijo	prefix, code
el abonado	the subscriber
oír/se oye	to hear/one hears, you hear
comunicando	engaged

Para estudiar

Oye, *to hear*

Notice the phrase **si se oye** *if one hears.* **Oye** is part of the verb **oír** *to hear.* The present tense forms are as follows:

I	oigo
you (tú)	oyes
he/she/it/you (Vd.)	oye
we	oímos
you (vosotros)	oís
they/you (Vds.)	oyen

You will see this is a little like the forms of **decir**, **seguir**, and **salir** that you met in Unit 14.

The form **oiga**, *listen!* is used if you are trying to get through on the phone and saying 'hello'. When you pick up a phone which is ringing you say **diga** (lit. *speak!*). **Oiga** is also used to attract someone's attention – a more polite form than 'pssst'.

Urgencias

Si no se sabe qué número marcar, se puede buscar en la guía. Aquí hay unos teléfonos útiles de la guía de Madrid.

Vds ven aquí los números que hay que marcar si se necesita un taxi, si hay un incendio, o si su coche tiene una avería, etc.

bomberos	firemen
RENFE	Red Nacional de Ferrocarriles Españoles – the Spanish National Railway Network
incendio	fire (an accidental fire – the more common word is **fuego**; a bonfire is **una hoguera**)
avería	breakdown

la policía	police (force) but
el policía	policeman
Similarly:	
la guía	guidebook, directory, guide
el guía	guide (if it's a man)

2 Look at this sentence, then complete the others in the same way.

Si hay un accidente, hay que llamar a la cruz roja.

Si hay un incendio, ...

Si hay un robo, ...

Si se quiere ir al teatro, ...

Si se quiere tomar un avión ....

Si hay una avería en el coche, ...

Si se quiere ir en tren, ...

Now go straight on to the next exercise, which will give you the answers.

Without looking at the above, do the same process with the phrases reversed. Here is a model:

Hay que llamar a la cruz roja si hay un accidente.

Hay que llamar a los bomberos ....

Hay que llamar a la policía ....

Hay que llamar a radio-taxi ....

Hay que llamar a IBERIA ....

Hay que llamar a ayuda carretera ....

Hay que llamar a la RENFE ....

Repeat these two exercises until you can do them both without cross-checking.

20

HABLANDO DEL TIEMPO

Talking about the weather

In this unit you will learn

- how to describe the weather
- the points of the compass

Lectura

Aquí hay un pronóstico del tiempo como se ve cada día en el periódico *(see the weather map on page 162)*.

Hoy llueve en el norte de España, y hace sol en el sur. Hay nubes y claros en el centro, el oeste y el este, y también en el noreste.

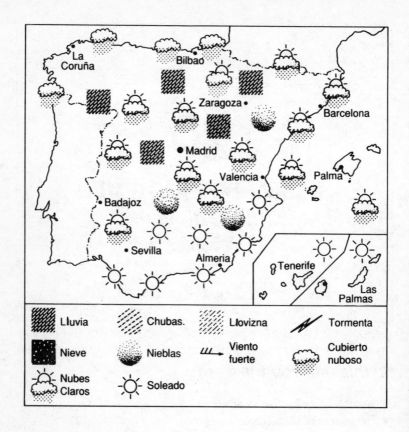

—— ¿Cómo es el tiempo en Abril? ——

Now look at the record, on page 163, of the weather one April, and read the description that follows.

El 1 y 2 de abril hay nubes y claros, pero el 3 llueve. Hay tormenta el 4, y dos días más de lluvia. El 7 y 8 caen chubascos, después sale el sol y hace sol cuatro días seguidos. El 14 está nuboso, y los nubes siguen hasta el día 16, cuando hace mucho viento; hay más lluvia el día 17. Después, el tiempo mejora un poco pero hace mal

1	2	3	4	5	6
7	8	9	10	11	12
13	14	15	16	17	18
19	20	21	22	23	24
25	26	27	28	29	30

tiempo el 23, 24, 25 y 26 cuando el cielo está cubierto, llueve y hay tormenta. Pero el mes de abril termina con buen tiempo y cuatro días de un sol espléndido.

lluvia	rain
chubascos	showers
llovizna	drizzle
tormenta	storm
nieve	snow
nieblas	fog
viento fuerte	strong winds
cubierto nuboso	cloud cover
nubes y claros	sunny periods
soleado	sunny
caer	to fall (see Unit 7)
llover	to rain
seguir	to continue, follow (see Unit 14)
mejorar	to improve
el cielo	the sky

Comentario

You can also say:

Hace calor, hace mucho calor.	*It is hot, very hot.*
Hace frío, hace mucho frío.	*It is cold, very cold.*
Hace (mucho) viento.	*It is (very) windy.*
Hace sol.	*It is sunny.*
Hace buen tiempo.	*It is fine.*
Hace mal tiempo.	*The weather is bad.*

Notice also:

Llueve	*It rains (in general).*
Está lloviendo.	*It is raining (now).*

Similarly:

Nieva en invierno.	*It snows in winter.*
No está nevando ahora.	*It is not snowing now.*

Actividad

1 Using the information in the weather record and description, answer the following questions in Spanish.

(a) ¿Qué tiempo hace el tres de abril?

(b) ¿Está lloviendo el día siete?

(c) ¿Cuándo sale el sol otra vez?

(d) ¿Hace calor el día cuatro?

(e) ¿Hace buen tiempo el dieciséis y diecisiete?

(f) ¿Hace mejor tiempo el día veinte o el veintiuno?

(g) ¿Cuándo hace peor (*worse*) tiempo, el veintidós o el veintitrés?

(h) ¿Cuántos días de sol hay este mes?

(i) ¿Cuántos días hay de lluvia intensa?

(j) ¿En qué días hay tormenta?

Comentario

On page 165, you can see the points of the compass in Spanish:

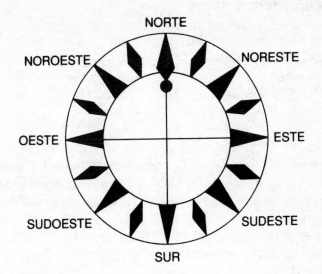

Actividad

2 The sentences below are based on the forecast shown on the weather map on page 162 . Look back at the map and fill in the gaps in each sentence.

(a) En Badajoz hay … y … pero en Sevilla … … .

(b) En el noroeste de España … … está … de nubes, y hay … también.

(c) Al norte y al sur de Madrid, hay … y … , pero al oeste y al noreste de la ciudad hay … .

(d) Las regiones del país donde está soleado son Las … , … , y el … .

(e) En Bilbao, no hace … tiempo – hay … … .

(f) Al oeste de Barcelona, y en en el sudeste del país, hay … , pero en la costa sudeste está … .

Para estudiar

Hace calor/tengo calor

Notice the difference between:

	Hace calor.	*It (the weather) is hot.*
	Hace frío.	*It is cold.*
and	**Tengo calor.**	*I am hot. (lit.* I have heat.*)*
	Tengo frío.	*I am cold.*
and	**El agua está caliente.**	*The water is hot.*
	El café está frío.	*The coffee is cold.*

In other words you use **hace** when saying that the weather is hot or cold, but you use **tengo** when saying that you, personally, are hot or cold. Similarly:

¿Tienes frío?	*Are you cold?*
Isabel tiene frío.	*Isabel is cold.*
En agosto tenemos calor.	*We are hot in August.*

Things or substances such as drinks, food, or metal simply *are* (**está/están**) hot (**caliente**) or cold (**frío**):

Esta cerveza no está fría.	*This beer isn't cold.*
Este chocolate está demasiado caliente	*This chocolate is too hot.*

21

PARA TERMINAR ...

And finally ...

Read this unit last, whatever the order in which you have studied the units 12 to 20. Here we try to put things in perspective for you, and fill in one or two of the inevitable gaps.

Firstly, as we have already mentioned, Spanish is not the only language you will hear in Spain. Look again at the map in Unit 15. In the north east, in Cataluña, you will hear Catalán and see street signs, shop names, etc. in Catalán. Similarly, at the other end of the Pyrenees, in the north west, you will hear and see Basque. All the inhabitants speak Spanish as well, of course. Also, as in most countries, there are local accents and dialects. The language you have read in this book and heard on the tapes is standard Spanish – Castilian – which is fundamentally the language of Old Castile, the area north of Madrid. Perhaps the clearest Spanish spoken by ordinary people is to be heard in the regions which centre on Burgos and Soria. In other regions, people speak with an accent, sometimes too slight for you to notice, elsewhere so extreme that it is difficult to understand people until you get used to the way they speak. Then again, just as with English, not everyone speaks very well. Some people gabble, some use slang, some are not very articulate. But nevertheless they will all, in general, make quite an effort to help you understand and to understand you. As we said in the **Introduction**, the Spanish are usually delighted that you have taken the trouble to learn some of their language and will go out of their way to be accommodating.

Secondly, you can learn a lot from the written language that you come across, such as signs and lettering you see in the street. Here are a few of the more common ones which may be of practical use.

Prohibiciones *Prohibitions*

No tocar	Do not touch
No fumar	No smoking
Perros no	No dogs allowed
No aparcar. Llamamos grúa.	No parking. Towaway in operation. (lit. we call the crane)
No tire colillas/papeles/basura	Do not drop cigarette ends/paper/rubbish
No pisar el césped	Keep off the grass
Privado	Private
Prohibido el paso	No entry

Instrucciones *Instructions*

Empujad/Tirad	Push/Pull (on doors)
Llamar	Ring (or knock) (for attention)
Introdúzcase la moneda en la ranura	Insert the money in the slot
Prepare la moneda exacta	Tender the correct fare
Peatón – circule por la izquierda	Pedestrian – walk on the left
P En batería	Parking (side by side)
P En línea (en cordón)	Parking (end to end)

Información *Information*

Entrada/Salida	Entrance/Exit
Sin salida	No exit
Abierto/Cerrado	Open/Closed
Cerrado por vacaciones	Closed for annual holiday
Cerrado por descanso del personal	Closed for staff holiday
No funciona	Out of order
Se vende	For sale
Agua potable (agua no potable)	Drinking water (non–drinking water)
Hecho a mano	Hand-made
De artesanía	Hand-made
No se admiten reclamaciones	Goods are non-returnable
Paso de peatones	Pedestrian crossing
Ambulatorio	Out-patients' clinic

Lastly, how much of the grammar of Spanish have we been able to cover in this book? Enough, we hope, to enable you to manage in relatively straightforward, practical situations. But of course there is a great deal which we have not explained, and which falls outside the aim of this particular course. Much of it is related to verbs. We have not included, for example, any means of indicating actions or events which have occurred in the past (except for a fleeting reference in Unit 16: **me he dado un golpe en la cabeza** *I have hurt my head*). Neither have we explained how to indicate events which will occur in the future. However, you can exploit one method of talking about the future by using the words for *go*. (See Unit 14.) Look at these examples:

Voy a comprar las entradas.	*I'm going to buy the tickets.*
Voy a ir.	*I'm going to go.*
Vamos a visitar el museo.	*We're going to visit the museum.*
Van a llegar mañana.	*They will arrive tomorrow.*

Other types of sentences are less simply conveyed in Spanish. You will have to follow a more advanced course than this in order to cope with sentences such as *If I had known, I should have come earlier*. In the same way, issuing commands – *give it to me, don't tell him so* – involves much practice, as we suggested in Unit 15. Even when you have mastered most or all of the formal grammar, there are many usages which seem to fall outside what is explained in the textbooks and dictionaries, especially in the everyday use of the language by Spaniards amongst themselves. But this can be an advantage, because you can acquire a good deal of language use by training yourself to *listen*, to note what the Spanish say in certain situations or to convey certain reactions, and by imitating them. Here are a few examples of common conversational phrases that are worth learning:

¡No me diga(s)!	You don't say! Well I never!
¡Vaya coche/casa! etc.	What a car/house! etc.
¡Vaya jaleo!	What a racket! (noise)
¡Vaya una cosa!	Well there's a thing!
Que le (te) vaya bien.	I hope things go well with you.
Me viene muy bien.	It's just right, it's very convenient, just what I wanted.
Me da igual.	I don't mind, it's all the same to me (see Unit 9).
Digo.	I mean (said when you have made a mistake and are correcting yourself)

¡Qué cosa más rara!	What a peculiar thing!
¡Qué cosa más fina! etc.	What a fine thing! etc.
¡Qué emoción!	How exciting!
¡Qué cara más dura!	What a sauce! What a cheek!
Desde luego.	Of course (agreeing with someone).
¡Qué lío!	What a mix-up!
¡Qué pena!	What a shame!
Me da vergüenza/me da corte	I feel embarrassed about it.
Es para volverse loco	It's enough to drive you mad.
No faltaría más.	By all means/please do.
No hay de qué/de nada.	Don't mention it/you're welcome.
En absoluto.	Not in the slightest.

¡**Vaya**! and ¡**anda**! are very common expressions and can be used in a variety of ways. For example ¡**anda**! can be a mild expression of surprise, a much stronger one if you drag out the last syllable ¡**andaaaa**!. To express disbelief you can repeat it rapidly and dismissively: **anda, anda, anda.** (Or **ande, ande, ande** if you are using **Vd.**) You need, though, to hear these expressions in action before you use them yourself.

This point returns us to what we said at the beginning, in the Introduction: language is above all a social activity. There is a limit to what you can usefully do on your own, and experts would disagree about where that limit is. What you need to do, now that you have worked through this book, is to use every opportunity to speak Spanish, in Spain if possible, but failing that, in a class with a group of other learners, or with a native speaker. ¡**Que le vaya bien!**

Clave

Key to the exercises

Unit 1

Actividades

2(a) Buenos días, señor (b) Hola *or possibly* Buenos días (c) Buenas tardes, señores (d) Hola (e) Buenas noches   **3**(a) Este señor es Paco. (b) Esta señorita es Isabel. (c) Esta señora es la señora Ortega. (d) Estos señores son los señores Herrero. (e) No, este señor no es Pedro, es Paco. (f) No, esta señorita no es Luisa, es Isabel. (g) No, estos señores no son los señores García, son los señores Alba. **4**(a) Estos señores son los señores Méndez, ¿no? (b) Este senōr es Paco, ¿no? (c) Esta señorita Juanita, ¿no? (d) ¿Es Vd. Paco? (e) ¿Son Vds. los señores Alba?   **5**(a)¿Cómo se llama Vd. (señor)? *or* ¿Quién es Vd. (señor)? (b)¿Cómo se llama? *or* ¿Quién es (esta señorita)? (c)¿Cómo se llama Vd. (señora)? *or* ¿Quién es Vd. (señora)? (d) ¿Cómo se llama? *or* ¿Quién es (este señor)? (e)¿Se llama Vd. Pedro (señor)? *or* ¿Vd. se llama Pedro, ¿no? *or* ¿Es Vd. Pedro (señor)? *or* Vd. es Pedro, ¿no? (f) Este señorita se llama Luisa, ¿no? (g) Vds. son los señores Ortega, ¿no?   **6**(a) me llamo (b) perdone (c) ¿quién es? (d) hola (e) hasta luego *Column A:* Adios   **Documento número 1:** Hotel San Nicolás

Evaluación

1¿Quién es Vd.? *or* ¿Cómo se llama Vd.?   **2** Me llamo… *or* Soy …
3 ¿Se llama Vd.…? *or* ¿Vd. es …?   **4** Perdone, señorita   **5** Estos señores son los señores Méndez.

Unit 2

Actividades

1 (a) Soy de (place name). (b) Soy inglés (inglesa), americano (americana), etc. (c) No soy español (española). (d) ¿Es Vd. español, Paco? (e) Isabel, ¿es Vd. española? (f) ¿De dónde es Vd., Isabel? (g) Señores Méndez, ¿de dónde son Vds? (h) ¿Son Vds. de Madrid, señores? (Sí, somos de Madrid.) (i) Señores Méndez, ¿son Vds. españoles? (Sí, somos españoles.) (j) Somos ingleses. (k) No somos españoles. **2** (a) Un sevillano es de Sevilla. Un madrileño es de Madrid. Un barcelonés es de Barcelona. (b) Un granadino es de Granada. Un cordobés es de Córdoba. Un malagueño es de Málaga.) (c) Un burgalés es de Burgos. Un zaragozano es de Zaragoza. Un tarraconense es de Tarragona. (d) Un toledano es de Toledo. Un salmantino es de Salamanca. Un vallisoletano es de Valladolid. (e) Un zamorano es de Zamora. Un conquense es de Cuenca. Un gaditano es de Cádiz. (f) Un donostiarra es de San Sebastián. **3** italiano, español, francés, inglés, catalán, ruso (Russian), danés (Danish) **4** (a) Sí, hablo inglés (b) Sí, soy americano, *or* No, soy… Vd. es catalán, ¿no? (c) No, no entiendo catalán. Hablo francés y español. (d) Muchas gracias. **5** (a) (iv), (b) (i), (c) (v), (d) (iii), (e) (ii) **Documento número 2:** Soy como soy.

Evaluación

1 Soy… (e.g. de Londres, de New York, de Canberra, madrileño/a, etc.) **2** Soy (e.g. inglés, americano, francés, australiano, etc.) **3** Hablo (e.g. inglés, francés, alemán, etc.) **4** Vd. habla inglés muy bien **5** ¿De dónde es Vd.? **6** ¿Es Vd. (e.g. español/española, inglés/inglesa, americano/americana, etc.)? **7** (a) español/española (b) escocés/escocesa (c) catalán/catalana (d) vasco/vasca (e) alemán/alemana

Unit 3

Actividades

1 (a) V (b) F (c) F (d) F (e) V (f) V **2** (a) Paco trabaja en una oficina de la calle Goya. (b) Paco vive en un apartamento en la calle Meléndez Valdés. (c) Isabel trabaja en las oficinas de IBERIA en la calle María de Molina. (d) Isabel vive con su familia en un piso en la calle Almagro. (e) No, Paco no vive en un piso grande, vive en un apartamento pequeño. (f) No, Isabel no vive en la calle Goya, vive en la calle Almagro. (g) Es Paco quien vive en la calle Meléndez Valdés. (h) Es Isabel quien trabaja en María de Molina. (i) No, Paco no trabaja como administrador, es arquitecto. (j) La oficina en María de Molina es de IBERIA – Líneas Aéreas de España. **3** (a) los (b) el (c) la (d) las (e) los (f) la (g) el **4** (a) un colegio (b) una oficina (c) un hospital (d) una oficina *or* un estudio (e) un teatro (f) un café **5** (a) ¿Dónde vive Vd., Paco? (Vivo en Meléndez Valdés, en un apartamento.) (b) ¿Dónde trabaja Vd., Isabel? (Trabajo en María de Molina, en la oficina de IBERIA). (c) Vivo también en un apartamento pequeño. (d) Trabajo en una oficina también. (e) No hablo muy bien el español todavía. (f) Soy inglés/inglesa (escocés/ escocesa, etc). Hablo inglés. **6** *Missing number –* siete. **Documento número 3:** (a) 4 (b) in a garage (c) during office hours

Evaluación

1 veinte, diecinueve, dieciocho, diecisiete, dieciséis, quince, catorce, trece, doce, once, diez, nueve, ocho, siete, seis, cinco, cuatro, tres, dos, uno, cero. **2** Paco vive en la calle Meléndez Valdés, número cinco, tercero D, en Madrid. **3** Isabel, ¿dónde vive Vd.? ¿Y dónde trabaja Vd.? **4** Soy director(a) de una empresa **5** Vivo... y trabajo ...

Unit 4

Actividades

1 Paco es español. Isabel es madrileña. Los señores Méndez están casados. El apartamento de Paco es pequeño. IBERIA es una compañía importante. Isabel y Paco son madrileños. El piso de Isabel es muy grande. La oficina de Paco está en la calle Goya **2** (a) no están (b) no es (c) no es (d) no está (e) no son (f) no están (g) no está (h) no son **3** (a) Está muy bien (b) No, está casada con Paul (c) Sí, naturalmente (d) Es muy simpático. Es escocés. (e) Viven en Edimburgo (f) Es contable y trabaja en Edimburgo (g) Sí, trabaja en una agencia de turismo **4** (a) Está muy bien (b) No está muy bien (c) Es arquitecto. (d) Está en casa (e) Está de vacaciones. (f) Está contento. (g) Es de Madrid. (h) Está en Madrid. (i) Es español. (j) Está constipado. **5** (a) Están muy bien. (b) No están muy bien. (c) Son simpáticos. (d) Están en casa. (e) Están de vacaciones. (f) Están contentos. (g) Son de Madrid. (h) Están en Madrid (i) Son españoles. (j) Están

constipados.   **Documento numero 4:** (a) El Tabernón (b) En Ávila
(c) La calle San Segundo

Evaluación

1 Estoy contento/a   **2** Estoy de vacaciones   **3** ¿Qué hace Vd. *or*
¿Dónde trabaja Vd.?   **4** Estoy casado/a, estoy soltero/a   **5** ¿Está
Paco?   **6** ¿Cómo está Vd.?   **7** Estoy bien. No estoy muy bien.

Unit 5

Actividades

1 (a) El padre de Luis es el señor Méndez. (b) Se llama Luis. (c) Se
llama Isabel. (d) Tiene cuatro abuelos. (e) Tiene un sobrino. (f) Los
señores Méndez son los suegros de Margarita. (g) Los señores
Ballester son los suegros de Luis. (h) Isabel es la cuñada de Luis. (i)
Se llama Fernando. (j) Luisito tiene dos tíos y una tía.   **2** (a) hermana
(b) hermanos (c) mi, mi cuñado (d) mis, abuelos (e) cuatro (f) mi, se
llama (g) mi, el hermano (h) cuatro, un (i) una hija (j) están,
tienen   **3** (a) Carlos López Silva (b) Carmen Rivera García (c) Ana
Serrano (d) Pedro López Rivera (e) Carmen López Rivera (f) Diego
López Rivera (g) María Ayala (h) Carmen López Serrano (i) Diego
López Ayala (j) José María López Ayala   **4** (a) pero Isabel no (b) pero
Isabel no (c) pero Isabel sí (d) pero Isabel sí (e) pero Isabel sí (f) pero
Isabel no   **5** (a) Hoy hay fabada en el restaurante. (b) En el quiosco
hay billetes de lotería. (c) No. Para el teatro no hay entradas. (d) Hay
cuatro vuelos diarios de la BA de Londres a Madrid. (e) Sí. El aparta-
mento de Paco es suficiente para él. (f) No es de él, está alquilado. (g)
Porque sus padres viven en Alicante. (h) El coche de Paco siempre
está en la calle. (i) El coche de la familia de Isabel es de sus padres. (j)
El perro en casa de Isabel es de su madre.

Unit 6

Actividades

1 (a) el uno de marzo (b) el dieciséis de junio (c) el treinta y uno de
agosto (d) el dos de noviembre (e) el cuatro de julio (f) el diecinueve
de mayo (g) el veintidós de febrero (h) el diez de abril (i) el veintiséis
de octubre (j) el veinticuatro de diciembre (k) el treinta de enero (l) el
once de noviembre   **3** (a) Voy a Santander. (b) Porque tengo un con-

greso en Santander. (c) No. En Barcelona tengo una reunión. (d) Voy el cinco de junio. (e) A Barcelona voy el día nueve. (f) Voy en coche. (g) Vuelvo a Madrid el diez de junio. (h) Porque voy directamente de Santander a Barcelona.   **4** (a) Estamos en Málaga porque estamos de vacaciones. (b) Volvemos a Madrid el día treinta. (c) Pasamos un mes en Málaga. (d) No. Tenemos un piso alquilado. (e) Vamos al café para tomar el aperitivo. (f) Sí. Vamos mañana también. (g) Sí. Vamos todos los días. (h) No. Volvemos a casa para comer. (i) No tenemos familia en Málaga, pero sí tenemos amigos. (j) Vamos al cine o al teatro.   **5** (a) Sí, voy a Santander y Madrid. (b) Voy el día veinte de julio. (c) Paso diez días en Santander, y después voy a Madrid. (d) Sí, paso cinco días en Madrid con mis amigos. (e) No, tomo el tren   **6** Para visitar las capitales de provincia se puede alquilar un coche. Para un aperitivo se puede tomar un gin-tonic. Para ir a Barcelona se puede tomar el tren, el avión, o el autobús. Para ir a Gerona en agosto se puede tomar un vuelo charter. Para pasar un mes en Málaga se puede alquilar un piso. Para visitar Venezuela se puede tomar un vuelo internacional de IBERIA. Para comer se puede ir a un restaurante. Para la digestión después de comer se puede dormir la siesta.   **Documento número 5:** (a) 19.500 ptas. (b) 52 (c) Fill in your name, address, post code, town, county, telephone number, signature, method of payment. **Documento número 6:** Servicios especiales de lujo (*special luxury service*), más rápidos (*faster*), más seguros (*safer*), más cómodos (*more comfortable*), que cualquier (*than any*) otro medio (*other means*) de transporte por carretera (*of road transport*) que Vd. pueda elegir (*that you can choose*).

Evaluación

1 Treinta y uno, treinta, veintinueve, veintiocho, veintisiete, veintiséis, veinticinco, veinticuatro, veintitrés, veintidós, veintiuno   **2** enero, febrero, marzo, abril, mayo, junio, julio, agosto, septiembre, octubre, noviembre, diciembre   **4** ¿Cómo se va al teatro?   **5** ¿Se habla inglés aquí?   **6** Se puede tomar el autobús a la estación.   **7** Hay cinco vuelos todos los días.   **8** Paso un mes en España todos los años.

Unit 7

Actividades

1 (a) El veintiuno cae en un martes. (b) El treinta y uno cae en un viernes. (c) El primer domingo cae en el día cinco. (d) El último domingo cae en el día veintiséis. (e) Los sábados en julio caen en el cuatro, el once, el dieciocho y el veinticinco. (f) El veintisiete cae en un lunes. (g) El cumpleaños de Isabel cae en un miércoles este año. (h) No. En julio el trece no cae en martes. **2** (a) domingo (b) miércoles (c) martes (d) jueves (e) sábado (f) viernes (g) lunes. *Column A*: octubre **3** (a) F (b) V (c) V (d) F (e) V (f) V (g) F (h) F (i) F (j) V **4** (a) a las ocho y media de la tarde (b) a las siete y media de la tarde (c) a las seis y veinticinco de la tarde (d) a las nueve y veinte de la mañana (e) a las nueve y cinco de la tarde (f) a las dos y cuarto de la tarde

Unit 8

Actividades

1 (b) Necesito salir a las ocho y media. (c) Quisiera hablar por teléfono a las diez y cuarto. (d) Necesito hablar con el director a las doce menos cuarto. (e) Quisiera comer a las dos. (f) Quisiera tomar un gin-tonic a la una y media. (g) Necesito estar en casa a las cinco. (h) Necesito ir al dentista a las cinco y media. (i) Quisiera las entradas para las siete y media de la tarde. (j) Quisiera hacer la reserva en el restaurante para las diez y media de la noche. (k) Necesito salir con el perro a las doce de la noche. **2** (a) F (b) F (c) F (d) V (e) F (f) V (g) V (h) F **3** (a) lo (b) las (c) los (d) lo (e) lo **Documento número 7:** (a) Para el 18 de agosto (b) 19L (c) no-fumadores (d) Madrid – Londres

Evaluación

1 Quisiera un café. **2** Necesito estar en Madrid el viernes. **3** Quiere hacer una reserva, por favor? **4** Necesito estar en la oficina para una reunión el día diecisiete. **5** Voy a París mañana. El vuelo sale a las diez y cuarto de la mañana. **6** Quisiera dos entradas de teatro, para el día veintitrés por favor.

Unit 9

Actividades

1 (a) no le gusta (b) quisiera (c) quiere (d) se llama (e) un ángel (f) le gusta (g) le gusta (h) demasiada política y demasiado fútbol (i) le gustan (j) son demasiado sentimentales (k) le gustan **2** (a) Me gusta el café. (b) Lo prefiero con leche. (c) No quiero azúcar. (d) No me apetece un café ahora. (e) ¿Quiere Vd. un té, Isabel? (f) ¿Cómo lo quiere? (g) ¿Lo prefiere siempre con leche? (h) ¿No le gusta el té con azúcar? (i) ¿Le gustan los vinos españoles, Paco? (j) ¿Prefiere Vd. el güisqui o el vermú? (k) ¿Le apetece un gin-tonic? (l) ¿Lo quiere con limón? **3** (a) No, no me apetece ir al cine (b) No, no me gusta el chocolate (c) No, no quiero un gin-tonic (d) No, no me gusta la música de Verdi (e) No, no me apetece salir en el coche (f) Sí, me apetece ir a casa. **4** (a) (vii), (b) (iii) (iv) (vi) (vii), (c) (i) (ii) (viii), (d) (i) (ii) (v) (viii) **Documento número 8:** (a) 155 ptas (b) 620 ptas (c) para el 8 de abril de 1991 (d) 15.51 h (a las cuatro menos diez) **Documento número 9...** (a) No, no quiero ir a Mallorca. (b) Sí, prefiero ir a Gran Canaria. (c) 2.000 Ptas. (d) 3.000 Ptas. (e) En Viajes Barceló (*Barceló Travel*).

Evaluación

1 Me gusta la música. **2** Me gusta mucho/muchísimo la música flamenca. **3** No me gusta el fútbol. **4** Prefiero la música clásica. **5** ¿Le gusta a Vd. la música flamenca? **6** ¿Prefiere Vd. la música flamenca o la música clásica? **7** Quiero ir a casa porque no me apetece trabajar más y necesito un gin-tonic.

Unit 10

Actividades

1 (a) A las siete Paco se levanta (b) Después, se lava y se viste. (c) Sale de casa a las ocho menos veinte. (d) Cuando llega a la oficina se sienta para trabajar. (e) Se siente bien porque tiene compañeros simpáticos. (f) No. Los Méndez se levantan tarde. (g) Porque no tienen prisa. No trabajan. (h) Antes de salir se lavan y se visten (se arreglan). (i) Cuando llegan al café se sientan en la terraza. (j) Dice que les gusta salir todos los días. **2** (a) ¿A qué hora se levanta Vd., Paco? (b) ¿A qué hora sale Vd. de casa? (c) ¿A qué hora llega Vd. a la oficina? (d) ¿Le gusta su trabajo? (e) ¿Por qué le gusta? (f) ¿A qué hora se levantan Vds? (g) ¿Por qué no tienen Vds. prisa? (h) ¿Por qué no trabaja su marido? (i) ¿A qué hora salen Vds? (j) ¿Dónde se sientan Vds. en el café? **3** (a) (ii), (b) (iii), (c) (ii), (d) (i), (e) (iii), (f) (ii) **4** (a) Se toma un aperitivo a las siete de la tarde. (b) Se come bien en España. (c) Se habla bien el español en Burgos. (d) Se siente más contento en casa que en la oficina (e) Se necesita trabajar mucho. (f) Se sale con el perro todos los días. (g) No se puede pagar con cheque. (h) En Inglaterra se bebe más té que vino. **Documento número 10:** A contract of employment, an immediate start, and hours of 8.30–1.30 and 2.30–5.30.

Evaluación

1 Paco tiene prisa. **2** Tenemos prisa. **3** Me visto a las siete y salgo a las ocho y media. **4** Me lo paso bien los sábados. **5** No me siento bien, quiero volver a casa. **6** ¿Se puede pagar con tarjeta de crédito? **7** Me levanto tarde todos los domingos. **8** No me gusta trabajar en la oficina, porque mis compañeros son antipáticos (*or* no son simpáticos).

Unit 11

Actividad

(a) Paco, eres madrileño, ¿no? (b) ¿Vas todos los días al café, Paco? (c) ¿Tienes un coche, Paco? (d) ¿Te gusta el fútbol, Paco? (e) ¿Tienes prisa por las mañanas, Paco? (f) Isabel, ¿dónde pasas tus vacaciones? (g) y ¿dónde prefieres vivir? (h) ¿Qué te apetece más, Isabel, un té o un café? (i) ¿Que familia tenéis, Isabel y Paco? (j) ¿A qué hora salís por la mañana, Paco e Isabel?

Unit 12

Actividades

2 (a) ¿Tienes un carnet? (un Documento Nacional de Identidad?) (b) ¿Cuál es el número? (c) ¿Cuándo caduca? (¿Cuál es la fecha de caducidad?) (d) ¿Tienes un permiso de conducir? (e) ¿Tienes un pasaporte? (f) ¿Usas tarjeta de crédito? (g) ¿Tienes seguro de accidente? (h) ¿Cuál es el número de la poliza? (i) ¿Dónde vives? (j) ¿Cuál es tu número de teléfono? (k) ¿Cuáles son tus apellidos? (l) ¿Cómo se escriben? **3** (a) (v), (b) (iii), (c) (vi), (d) (ii), (e) (i), (f) (iv) **4** (a) quinientas pesetas (b) mil doscientas treinta y ocho pesetas (c) ciento sesenta y cuatro pesetas (d) cien pesetas (e) dos mil quinientas pesetas (f) cincuenta mil pesetas (g) docientas pesetas (h) mil novecientos noventa y cinco (i) mil novecientos ochenta y cuatro (j) dos mil diez (k) seis, cuarenta y nueve, diez (l) cuarenta y ocho, setenta y tres, veintiséis **Documento número 11:** (a) January to July (b) 9 (cantidades en miles de millones de pesetas)

Evaluación
1 Mi fecha de nacimiento es... 2 Mi apellido es... 3 Mi dirección es... 4 Mi número de pasaporte es... 5 Tengo seguro de accidente – el número de la poliza es... 6 Quisiera pagar con tarjeta de crédito.

Unit 13

Documento número 12: The Marbella apartments are right beside the beach. (**en primera línea** literally means *in the front line*.)

Unit 14

Actividades

1 (a) A Isabel no le interesa mucho el deporte. El señor Méndez es demasiado viejo. (b) A Isabel le gusta muchísimo la música. Al señor Méndez le gusta el fútbol. (c) Isabel toca el piano y la guitarra y va a muchos conciertos. El señor Méndez ve los partidos de fútbol en la televisión. (d) Isabel va al teatro con Paco y otros amigos. El señor Méndez va con su señora. (e) Isabel sale a museos y galerías. Los señores Méndez salen al café. 2 (a) (xii), (b) (viii), (c) (v), (d) (xviii), (e) (ii), (f) (xiii), (g) (iii), (h) (i) (xv), (i) (vi), (j) (iv) (xi) (xx), (k) (vii), (l) (ix) (xvii) (xix), (m) (x), (n) (xiv) (xvi) 3 (a) Está en la calle Fuencarral, número setenta y ocho. (b) No es necesario pagar – la entrada es gratuita. (c) La entrada tiene el número trescientos sesenta y dos mil, novecientos treinta y siete. (d) La entrada es para el uno de enero de mil novecientos noventa y uno. (e) Es para la función de la tarde. (f) La butaca está en la fila número siete (la séptima fila). **Documento número 13:** (a) Dos copias por el precio de una. (*Two copies for the price of one.*) (b) Sí, me gusta. (c) No, no hago muchas.

Unit 15

Actividades

1 (a) Sí. Hay un aparcamiento cerca del museo. (b) Está en la calle Trafalgar. (c) Frente a la iglesia hay un banco. (d) El mercado está en la calle Raimundo Lulio. (e) Sí. La farmacia está frente a Correos, al otro lado de la plaza. (f) No. El teatro está al otro lado de la calle Luchana. (g) Se toma la calle Raimundo Lulio y se sigue hasta el final. (h) La estación de metro está más cerca del cine. (i) El banco está en

la esquina de la calle Santa Engracia con la calle Santa Feliciana. **2** NB there are other routes and other ways of explaining them – if in doubt, check with the material in the dialogues. (a) Cruza esta calle aquí a la izquierda, y sigue hasta la plaza. Correos está a la izquierda. (b) Siga a la derecha por esta calle hasta la plaza, y el museo está a su izquierda. (c) Sí, en la Plaza de Chamberí. Tome la calle Raimundo Lulio enfrente, siga hasta el final, y hay una farmacia al otro lado de la plaza. (d) Toma la tercera calle aquí a la izquierda – la calle Sagunto, después del banco – y el cine está en tu derecha. **3** (a) Para ir desde Madrid a Cádiz, hay que tomar la carretera nacional cuatro. No. No se pasa por Granada. (b) Si se va desde Madrid a Portugal, se cruza la frontera cerca de Badajoz. (c) No. No hay mucha distancia entre Gijón y Oviedo. (d) Sí. Toledo está cerca de Madrid. (e) Valencia está más cerca de Madrid que Barcelona. (f) Para ir desde Francia a Alicante se toma el autopista. (g) Entre Badajoz y Gijón hay las ciudades de Cáceres, Salamanca, Zamora y Oviedo. (h) España es mucho más grande que Portugal. (i) Santiago está en Galicia. **4** (a) Sí, las carreteras son buenas, pero las distancias son grandes. (b) Sí, y me gustan los horizontes lejanos. (c) Hace calor en mayo, pero en julio, agosto y septiembre hace un calor intenso y es insoportable pasar todo el día en el coche. (d) Sí, hay, pero son de peaje, y prefiero las carreteras más pequeñas. Sin embargo, me gusta la autopista que conecta Bilbao y Barcelona. (e) En mayo no, pero sin embargo se necesita conducir con precaución y no ir demasiado rápido. En julio y agosto hay demasiadas coches porque millones de familias españolas se desplazan para sus vacaciones.

Unit 16

Actividades

1 (a) Hola, Ignacio. ¿Cómo estás? (b) ¿Tienes un catarro? (¿Estás constipado?) (c) ¿Tienes fiebre? (d) Dice treinta y siete grados. No tienes fiebre. (e) ¿Te duele la cabeza? (f) ¿Y te duele el estómago? (g) Tú no te sientes bien porque bebes demasiado. **Documento número 14:** Virgo, con diez estrellas. **2** (a) ¿Tienen Vds. una loción para una quemadura del sol? (b) Tengo un corte en el pie. ¿Tiene Vd. una pomada antiséptica y una venda? (c) Me duele el estómago. (d) Me duele una muela. ¿Tiene Vd. un analgésico? (e) Mi hijo no se siente bien y tiene fiebre. (f) Quiero unas gotas para un ojo inflamado. (g) Tengo el tobillo hinchado; necesito una tobillera. (h) Necesito ver a un médico. ¿Cuáles son las horas de consulta?   **3** (a) El medicamento se llama 'Anginovag'. (b) No es medicina, es un spray. (c) El envase tiene veinte mililitros (20 ml). (d) El tratamiento es para infecciones de la boca y la garganta. (e) La dosis preventiva es de una aplicación cada seis horas. (f) La dosis curativa es de una o dos aplicaciones cada dos o tres horas. (g) No hay efectos secundarios. (h) El medicamento se fabrica en Laboratorios Novag, S.A., que están en San Cugat del Vallés, cerca de Barcelona.

Unit 17

Actividades

1 '¿Nada más, señora? Pues son dos kilos de naranjas, a setenta y cinco el kilo, ciento cincuenta pesetas; cuarto de limones, cuarenta y cinco pesetas; un kilo de peras, cien pesetas; medio de fresas, ciento veinte pesetas; patatas, ochenta pesetas; medio de acelgas, sesenta y cinco pesetas; la lechuga, noventa y cinco pesetas; y los tomates, sesenta; ajos, cuarenta. Vamos a ver, cinco, diez, quince. Llevamos una. Cuatro y una, cinco; y seis, once: y nueve, veinte, y seis, veintiséis; y ocho, treinta y cuatro; y dos, treinta y seis; y cuatro, cuarenta; y cinco, cuarenta y cinco. Llevamos cuatro. Cinco, seis y siete. Setecientos cincuenta y cinco en total, señora.'   **2** (a) dos kilos de naranjas (b) doscientos gramos de jamón (c) un litro de leche (d) ciento cincuenta gramos de queso (e) dos ajos (f) un kilo de patatas (g) un cuarto de gambas (h) tres rajas de salmón   **3** (a) ¿Dónde está el departamento de perfumería? (b) ¿Tienen Vds. una farmacia? (c) ¿Dónde está la cafetería? (d) Quisiera pagar con Visa. (e) Voy a pagar en efectivo. (f) ¿En qué planta está la sección de deportes? (g) ¿Dónde están los aseos? (h) La librería está en la planta baja.   **Documento número 15:** (a) de creme tropical (b) 200 Grs. (c) en lugar fresco y seco.

Unit 18

Actividades

1 (a) Tengo hambre. (b) ¿Qué hay para comer? (c) ¿Tienes hambre? (d) A mí me gustan las pizzas. (e) ¿Te apetece una pizza? (f) ¿Prefieres pizza de anchoas o pizza de jamón? (g) Voy a llamar para una pizza. (h) ¿Quieres cerveza o Coca Cola? (i) Voy a comprar dos cervezas. (j)

Voy a tomar un café. **2** (a) (iii), (b) (ii), (c) (ii), (d) (ii), (e) (i), (f) (iii) **3 Tu:** (a) ¿Quieres un café? (b) ¿Quieres té con limón? (c) ¿Te apetece tarta de chocolate? (d) Te apetece tostada con miel? (e) ¿Quieres una cerveza fría? **Vd.:** (a) ¿Quiere Vd. un café? (b) ¿Quiere Vd. té con limón? (c) ¿Le apetece tarta de chocolate? (d) ¿Le apetece tostada con miel? (e) ¿Quiere una cerveza fría? **4** (a) Quisiera las judías. (b) Me gusta el pollo, pero no el ajo … Voy a tomar la merluza. (c) De postre quiero helado. (d) Prefiero chocolate. (e) Sin gas, por favor. (f) Con el pescado, tal vez blanco. (g) No quiero café, si no está incluido. **5** (a) Los entremeses, ¿qué son? (b) ¿Está fresca la merluza? (c) ¿Tiene mucho ajo el pollo? (d) ¿Qué fruta hay? (e) ¿El vino es de La Rioja? (f) ¿Se puede tomar cerveza en vez de vino?

Documento número 16: (a) beers, spirits, special coffees, pancakes, hot tapas (snacks), and sandwiches (b) from 9am to 1am.

Unit 19

Actividades

1 (a) ¿Se puede cambiar dinero en el hotel? (b) Quiero cambiar cien libras esterlinas. (c) ¿A cuánto está la libra? (d) Prefiero ir a un banco. (e) ¿A qué hora se cierra el banco? (f) Tengo que ir al banco antes de las dos. (g) Tengo cheques de viaje en dólares. (h) ¿Dónde está la caja? (i) ¿Dónde puedo comprar sellos? (j) Quiero dos sellos para cartas por avión a los Estados Unidos, y cinco sellos para postales para Inglaterra. (k) Tengo que echar las cartas hoy. (l) ¿Dónde está el buzón más cercano? (m) ¿Dónde están los aseos? (¿Dónde está el guardarropas?) **Documento número 17:** (**Sin comisiones:** *no commission*; **sin retención fiscal:** *no tax deduction*.

Unit 20

Actividades

1 (a) El tres de abril llueve. (b) Sí. El día siete caen chubascos. (c) El sol sale otra vez el diez. (d) No. El día cuatro no hace calor. Hay tormenta. (e) No. El dieciséis y diecisiete hace mal tiempo. (f) Hace mejor tiempo el veintiuno que el día veinte. (g) Hace peor tiempo el veintitrés porque el cielo está completamente cubierto. (h) Hay ocho días de sol este mes. (i) Hay cinco días de lluvia intensa. (j) Hay tormenta el día cuatro y el día veinticinco. **2** (a) nubes, claros, hace sol (b) el cielo, cubierto, lluvia (c) nubes, claros, lluvia (d) Palmas, Tenerife, sur (e) buen, cubierto nuboso (f) nieblas, soleado

Vocabulary

The following two lists contain the important words that have been used in this book, particularly those that have occurred more than once and in the exercises, plus a few extra useful words, especially in the English-Spanish list. What are not included are groups of words such as numbers, days, months, etc. which you will find easily in the text.

Try to look at the vocabulary lists just to jog your memory when you have forgotten a word – it is the **Subject Index** you should use to find your way back to more detailed explanations of usage.

Spanish–*English*

abierto *open*
abrigo (el) *(top) coat*
abuela (la) *grandmother*
abuelo (el) *grandfather*
abuelos (los) *grandparents*
afortunadamente *fortunately, luckily*
agradable *pleasant*
ahora *now*
albaricoque (el) *apricot*
algo *something, somewhat*
algunas veces *sometimes*
allá, más allá de *there, beyond*
almohada (la) *pillow*
almuerzo (el) *lunch (formal)*
alquiler *to rent, hire*
alquilar (el) *rent*
alto *tall*
amarillo *yellow*
ambiente (el) *atmosphere, surroundings*
amigo (el) (la amiga) *friend*
animado *lively*

año (el) *year*
antes (de) *before*
apellido (el) *surname*
apto *suitable*
aquí *here*
arreglar *to arrange*
armario (el) *cupboard*
autobús (el) *bus, coach*
autopista (la) *motorway*
avión (el) *aeroplane*
azúcar (el) *sugar*
azúl *blue*

bajo *short (people), low*
baño *bath*
barato *cheap*
barrio (el) *district (of town)*
bastante *enough, fairly*
beber *to drink*
bien *well*
billete (el) *ticket, banknote*

blanco *white*
blusa (la) *blouse*
bolsa (la) *bag*
bolso (el) *handbag*
botella (la) *bottle*
brazo (el) *arm*
bueno *good*
buscar *look for, search for*
butaca (la) *armchair*
buzón (el) *letterbox*

cabeza (la) *head*
cada e*ach, every*
caer t*o fall*
cajón (el) *drawer*
calcetines (los) *socks*
caliente *hot*
calle (la) *street*
calor (el) *heat*
calzoncillos (los) *(under) pants*
cama (la) *bed*
cambiar *to change*
caro *dear, expensive*
carretera (la) *road, main road*
carta (la) *letter (correspondence)*
casa (la) *house, home*
casado *married*
casi *almost*
cena (la) *supper, dinner*
cepillo de dientes (el) *(tooth)brush*
cerca (de) *near*
cerrado *closed, shut*
cielo (el) *sky*
cine (el) *cinema*
ciruela (la) *plum*
coche (el) *car*
cocina (la) *kitchen*
comedor (el) *dining room*
comer *to eat*
comida (la) *meal, main midday meal*
como *how*
compañero (la compañera) (el)
      colleague, companion
compañía (la) *company*
comprar *buy, to buy*
concierto (el) *concert*
conferencia (la) *trunk call*
congreso (el) *conference*

conocer *to know (people)*
contento *pleased, happy*
Correos *Post Office*
corto *short*
cuando *when*
cuanto, cuanta *how much*
cuantos, cuantas *how many*
cuarto de baño (el) *bathroom*
cuchara (la) *spoon*
cucharilla (la) *teaspoon*
cuchillo (el) *knife*
cuello (el) *neck*
cumpleaños (el) *birthday*
champú (el) *shampoo*
chaqueta (la) *jacket*
chica (la) *girl*

dar *to give*
de *of, from*
de acuerdo *agreed*
débil *weak*
decir *to say*
demasiado, demasiada *too much*
demasiados, demasiadas *too many*
deporte (el) *sport*
derecha *right*
desayuno (el) *breakfast*
describir *to describe*
desde *since, from*
despacio *slowly*
después (de) *after*
día (el) *day*
diente (el) *tooth (incisor)*
difícil *difficult*
dinero (el) *money*
dirección (la) *address, direction*
divertir, divertirse *to amuse, to enjoy
      oneself*
doblar *to turn (corner), to fold*
donde *where*
dormitorio (el) *bedroom*
ducha (la) *shower*
duda, sin duda (la) *doubt, without
      doubt*

echar *to throw*
edredón (el) *duvet*
efectivo, en efectivo (el) *in cash*

ejemplo, por ejemplo (el) *example, for example*
empezar *to begin*
enfrente *opposite*
entrada (la) *ticket (entrance)*
escoger *to choose*
escribir *to write*
espalda (la) *back*
esquina (la) *corner (external)*
estanco (el) *kiosk (tobacco and stamps)*
este, esta *this*
estómago (el) *stomach*
estos, estas *these*
estudiante (la estudiante) (el) *student*
exposición (la) *exhibition*

fácil *easy*
falda (la) *skirt*
familia (la) *family*
fecha (la) *date*
fin (el) *end*
fin de semana (el) *weekend*
frente a *facing, opposite*
frío (el) *cold*
frío *cold (adjective)*
fuerte *strong*
función (la) *performance*
fútbol (el) *football*

golpe (el) *blow, knock*
grande *big, large, great*
gris *grey*

hablar *to speak*
hacer *to do, to make*
hasta *until*
hay *there is, there are*
hermana (la) *sister*
hermano (el) *brother*
higo (el) *fig*
hija (la) *daughter*
hijo (el) *son, child*
hijos (los) *children (relationship)*
hombre (el) *man*
hora (la) *time (of day)*
horario (el) *timetable*
hoy *today*

ida y vuelta *return (ticket)*
ida, de ida sólo *single, one way (ticket)*
idioma (el) *language*
interesante *interesting*
invierno (el) *winter*
ir *to go*
izquierda *left*

jabón (el) *soap*
jérez, vino de Jérez *sherry*
jóven *young*
jugar *to play (games)*

lado (el) *side*
largo *long*
lavabo (el) *washbasin*
lavar, lavarse *to wash, to wash oneself*
leche (la) *milk*
levantarse *to get up*
libra (la) *pound (sterling)*
limón (el) *lemon*
luz (la) *light, electricity*
llamar *to call*
llegar *to arrive*
llevar *to take, carry, wear*
lluvia (la) *rain*

madre (la) *mother*
madrileño *of Madrid*
malo *bad*
mañana, pasado mañana *tomorrow, the day after tomorrow*
mañana (la) *morning*
mandar *to send*
mano (la) *hand*
manzana (la) *apple*
manta (la) *blanket*
mapa (el) *map*
máquina de afeitar (la) *razor*
marido (el) *husband*
mariscos (los) *seafood, shellfish*
marrón *brown*
medias (las) *stockings*
médico (el) *doctor*
melocotón (el) *peach*
menos mal *just as well*
merienda (la) *tea (meal), picnic*
mes (el) *month*

mesa (la) *table*
mismo *same*
mostrar *to show*
muchas veces *often*
muela (la) *tooth (molar)*
mujer (la) *woman, wife*
museo (el) *museum*
muy *very*

nacimiento (el) *birth*
nacionalidad (la) *nationality*
nada *nothing*
nadie *nobody*
nadar *to swim*
naranja (la) *orange*
naturalmente *naturally, of course*
necesitar *to need*
negro *black*
nieta (la) *granddaughter*
nieto (el) *grandson*
ninguno *none*
niños (los) *children (age group)*
noche (la) *night*
nombre (el) *name, forename*
nuevo *new*
nunca *never*

oficina (la) *office*
oir *to hear*
ojo (el) *eye*
otoño (el) *autumn*
otro *other*

padre (el) *father*
padres (los) *parents*
pagar *to pay*
palabra (la) *word*
pantalones (los) *trousers*
pantis (los) *tights*
para *for, in order to*
parte, todas partes *part, everywhere*
partido (el) *match (sport)*
pasaporte (el) *passport*
pasar *to pass*
pasta de dientes (la) *toothpaste*
pata (la) *leg (animal)*
peaje (el) *toll (motorway toll)*
peine (el) *comb*

pequeño *small, little*
pera (la) *pear*
periódico (el) *newspaper*
pero *but*
perro (el) *dog*
pie (el) *foot*
piel (la) *skin*
pierna (la) *leg (human)*
piscina (la) *swimming pool*
piso (el) *flat*
planta (la) *storey, floor*
plátano (el) *banana*
plato (el) *plate*
plaza (la) *square*
pocas veces *not often*
poder *to be able to*
poner *to put*
por *through, by, along, (for)*
¿por qué? *why*
porque *because*
postre (el) *dessert*
preferir *to prefer*
pregunta (la) *question*
preguntar *to ask*
primavera (la) *spring*
primero (primer) *first*
primo (la prima) (el) *cousin*
prisa, tener prisa *to be in a hurry*
problema (el) *problem*
puerta *door*

que *which, that*
querer *to want, love*
quien, quienes *who*

rápido *fast, quick*
reunión (la) *meeting*
rincón (el) *corner (internal)*
rojo *red*

sábana (la) *sheet*
saber *to know (facts)*
sacar *to take out (of container)*
salir *to leave, go out*
salón *sitting room*
salvo *except*
seguir *to follow*
seguro *sure, certain*

seguro (el) *insurance*
sello (el) *stamp (postal)*
semana (la) *week*
sentarse *to sit down*
sentirse *to feel*
servilleta (la) *napkin*
siempre *always*
silla (la) *chair*
simpático *friendly, agreeable*
sino (no ... sino) *not ... but*
sobrina (la) *niece*
sobrino (el) *nephew*
sofá (la) *sofa*
sol (el) *sun*
soltera *spinster, single*
soltero *bachelor, single*

también *also, too*
tarde (la) *afternoon, evening*
tarde *late*
tarjeta (la) *card*
taza (la) *cup*
teatro (el) *theatre*
teléfono (el) *telephone*
temprano *early*
tenedor (el) *fork*
tener *to have*
tener que *to have to*
terraza (la) *terrace, cafe terrace*
tía (la) *aunt*
tiempo (el) *time, weather*
tinto *red (of wine)*
tío (el) *uncle*
toalla (la) *towel*
tocar *to touch, to play (instruments)*
todavía *still, yet*
todo, toda, todos, todas *all, every*
tomar *to take*

trabajar *to work*
trabajo (el) *work*
tren (el) *train*

último *last*
útil *useful*
uvas (las) *grapes*

vacación, estar de vacaciones (la) *holiday, to be on holiday*
valor (el) *value*
vaso (el) *tumbler*
veces, de vez en cuando (las) *times, from time to time*
ventana (la) *window (house)*
ventanilla (la) *window (kiosk, bank, etc.)*
ver *to see*
verano (el) *summer*
verdad (la) *truth*
verde *green*
vestir, vestirse *to get dressed*
viajar *to travel*
viaje (el) *journey*
viajero (el) *traveller*
vida (la) *life*
viejo *old*
viento (el) *wind*
vino (el) *wine*
visitar *to visit*
vivir *to live*
volver *to return*
vuelo (el) *flight*

y *and*

zapatos (los) *shoes*
zumo de fruta (el) *fruit juice*

English – *Spanish*

address *la dirección*
aeroplane *el avión*
after *después (de)*
afternoon *la tarde*
agreed *de acuerdo*
all, every *todo, toda, todos, todas*

almost *casi*
along *por*
also, too *también*
always *siempre*
amuse, to enjoy oneself *divertir, divertirse*

and *y*
apple *la manzana*
apricot *el albaricoque*
arm *el brazo*
armchair *la butaca*
arrange, to arrange *arreglar*
arrive, to arrive *llegar*
ask, to ask (a question) *preguntar*
atmosphere, surroundings *el ambiente*
aunt *la tía*
autumn *el otoño*

bachelor, single *soltero*
back *la espalda*
bad *malo*
bag *la bolsa*
banana *el plátano*
banknote *el billete*
bath *el baño*
bathroom *el cuarto de baño*
be able to, to be able to *poder*
because *porque*
bed *la cama*
bedroom *el dormitorio*
beer *la cerveza*
before *antes (de)*
begin, to begin *empezar*
beyond *más allá de*
big, large, great *grande*
birth *el nacimiento*
birthday *el cumpleaños*
blanket *la manta*
blouse *la blusa*
blow, knock *el golpe*
blue *azul*
bottle *la botella*
breakfast *el desayuno*
brother *el hermano*
brush *el cepillo*
bus, coach *el autobús*
but *pero*
buy, to buy *comprar*
by *por*

call, to call *llamar*
car *el coche*
card *la tarjeta*
carry, to carry *llevar*

in cash *en efectivo*
chair *la silla*
change, to change *cambiar*
cheap *barato*
children (age group) *los niños*
children (relationship) *los hijos*
choose, to choose *escoger*
cinema *el cine*
closed, shut *cerrado*
coat *el abrigo*
cold *el frío*
cold (adjective) *frío*
comb *el peine*
companion *el compañero (la compañera)*
company *la compañía*
concert *el concierto*
conference *el congreso*
congratulations *felicidades*
corner (external) *la esquina*
corner (internal) *el rincón*
corridor *el pasillo*
course, of course *naturalmente, desde luego*
cousin *el primo (la prima)*
cup *la taza*
cupboard *el armario*

date *la fecha*
daughter *la hija*
day *el día*
dear, expensive *caro*
describe, to describe *describir*
dessert *el postre*
difficult *difícil*
dining room *el comedor*
dinner *la cena*
direction *la dirección*
district (of town) *el barrio*
do, make, to do, to make *hacer*
doctor *el médico*
dog *el perro*
door *la puerta*
doubt, without doubt *la duda, sin duda*
drawer *el cajón*
dress, to get dressed *vestir, vestirse*
drink, to drink *beber*
duvet *el edredón*

each, every *cada*
early *temprano*
easy *fácil*
eat, to eat *comer*
electricity *la luz, la electricidad*
end *el fin*
enough *bastante*
evening *la tarde*
everywhere *en todas partes*
example, for example *el ejemplo, por ejemplo*
except *salvo*
exhibition *la exposición*
eye *el ojo*

facing *frente a*
fairly *bastante*
fall, to fall *caer*
family *la familia*
fast, quick *rápido*
father *el padre*
feel, to feel *sentirse*
fig *el higo*
first *primero (primer)*
flat *el piso*
flight *el vuelo*
floor (ground) *el suelo*
floor (storey) *la planta*
follow, to follow *seguir*
foot *el pie*
football *el fútbol*
for *para (sometimes 'por')*
fork *el tenedor*
fortunately, luckily *afortunadamente*
friend *el amigo (la amiga)*
friendly, agreeable *simpático*
from *de, desde*
fruit juice *el zumo de fruta*

get up, to get up *levantarse*
girl *la chica*
give, to give *dar*
glass el *vaso (tumbler), la copa (stemmed)*
go out, to go out *salir*
go, to go *ir*
good *bueno*
granddaughter *la nieta*

grandfather *el abuelo*
grandmother *la abuela*
grandparents *los abuelos*
grandson *el nieto*
grapes *las uvas*
green *verde*

hand *la mano*
handbag *el bolso*
have to, to have to *tener que*
have, to have *tener*
head *la cabeza*
hear, to hear *oír*
heat *el calor*
here *aquí*
holiday, to be on holiday *la vacación, estar de vacaciones*
home *la casa*
hot *caliente*
house *la casa*
how *como*
how many *cuántos, cuántas*
how much *cuánto, cuánta*
hurry, to be in a hurry *prisa, tener prisa*
husband *el marido*

insurance *el seguro*
interesting *interesante*

jacket *la chaqueta*
journey *el viaje*
just as well *menos mal*

kiosk (tobacco and stamps) *el estanco*
kitchen *la cocina*
knife *el cuchillo*
know, to know (facts) *saber*
know, to know (people) *conocer*

language *el idioma*
large *grande*
last *último*
late *tarde*
lavatory *el water (in a house)*
leave, to leave *salir*
left *izquierda*
leg (animal) *la pata*

leg (human) *la pierna*
lemon *el limón*
letter (correspondence) *la carta*
letterbox *el buzón*
life *la vida*
light, electricity *la luz*
live, to live *vivir*
lively *animado*
look for, search for *buscar*
long *largo*
love, to love (of people) *querer*
low *bajo*
lunch (formal) *el almuerzo*

Madrid, of Madrid *madrileño*
make, to make *hacer*
man *el hombre*
map *el mapa*
married *casado*
match (sport) *el partido*
meal, main midday meal *la comida*
meeting *la reunión*
milk *la leche*
mineral water *el agua mineral*
money *el dinero*
month *el mes*
morning *la mañana*
mother *la madre*
motorway *la autopista*
museum *el museo*

name, forename *el nombre*
napkin *la servilleta*
nationality *la nacionalidad*
naturally *naturalmente*
near *cerca (de)*
neck *el cuello*
need, to need *necesitar*
nephew *el sobrino*
never *nunca*
new *nuevo*
newspaper *el periódico*
niece *la sobrina*
night *la noche*
nobody *nadie*
none *ninguno*
not ... but *sino (no...sino)*
not often *pocas veces*

nothing *nada*
now *ahora*

of *de*
office *la oficina*
often *muchas veces*
old *viejo*
open *abierto*
opposite *enfrente*
orange *la naranja*
order, in order to *para*
other *otro*

parents *los padres*
pass, to pass *pasar*
passport *el pasaporte*
pay, to pay *pagar*
peach *el melocotón*
pear *la pera*
performance *la función*
picnic *la merienda*
pillow *el almohada*
plate *el plato*
play, to play (games) *jugar*
play, to play (instruments) *tocar*
pleasant *agradable*
pleased, happy *contento*
plum *la ciruela*
Post Office *Correos*
pound (sterling) *la libra*
prefer, to prefer *preferir*
problem *el problema*
put, to put *poner*

question *la pregunta*

rain *la lluvia*
raincoat *el impermeable*
razor *la máquina de afeitar*
red *rojo*
red (of wine) *tinto*
rent, the rent *el alquiler*
rent, to rent, hire *alquilar*
return (ticket) *ida y vuelta*
return, to return *volver*
right *derecha*
road, main road *la carretera*
same *mismo*

say, to say *decir*
seafood, shellfish *los mariscos*
see, to see *ver*
send, to send *mandar*
shampoo *el champú*
sheet *la sábana*
sherry *Jérez, vino de Jérez*
shirt *la camisa*
shoes *los zapatos*
short (people) *bajo*
short *corto*
show, to show *mostrar*
shower *la ducha*
side *el lado*
since *desde*
single, one way (ticket) *ida, de ida sólo*
sister *la hermana*
sit down, to sit down *sentarse*
sitting room *el salón*
skirt *la falda*
skin *la piel*
sky *el cielo*
slowly *despacio*
small, little *pequeño*
soap *el jabón*
socks *los calcetines*
sofa *la sofá*
something, somewhat *algo*
sometimes *algunas veces*
son *el hijo*
speak, to speak *hablar*
spinster, single *soltera*
sponge *la esponja*
spoon *la cuchara*
sport *el deporte*
spring *la primavera*
square *la plaza*
stairs *el escalera*
stomach *el estómago*
street *la calle*
strong *fuerte*
student *la estudiante (la estudiante)*
sugar *el azúcar*
suitable *apto*
summer *el verano*
sun *el sol*
sun-tanned skin *la piel morena*
supper, dinner *la cena*

sure, certain *seguro*
surname *el apellido*
swim, to swim *nadar*
swimming pool *la piscina*

table *la mesa*
take out (of container) *sacar*
take, to take *llevar, tomar*
tall *alto*
tea (meal) *la merienda*
teaspoon *la cucharilla*
telephone *el teléfono*
terrace, cafe terrace *la terraza*
that (which) *que*
theatre *el teatro*
there *allá*
there is, there are *hay*
these *estos, estas*
through *por*
throw, to throw *echar*
ticket (entrance) *la entrada*
ticket (transport) *el billete*
tights *los pantis*
time *el tiempo*
time (of day) *la hora*
from time to time *a veces, de vez en cuando*
timetable *el horario*
today *hoy*
toll (motorway toll) *el peaje*
tomorrow, the day after tomorrow *mañana, pasado mañana*
too many *demasiados, demasiadas*
too much *demasiado, demasiada*
tooth (incisor) *el diente*
tooth (molar) *la muela*
toothbrush *el cepillo de dientes*
toothpaste *la pasta de dientes*
touch, to touch *tocar*
towel *la toalla*
train *el tren*
travel, to travel *viajar*
traveller *el viajero*
trousers *los pantalones*
trunk call *la conferencia*
truth *la verdad*
turn (corner), to fold *doblar*
uncle *el tío*

underpants *los calzoncillos*
until *hasta*
useful *útil*

value *el valor*
very *muy*
visit, to visit *visitar*
want, to want *querer*
wash, to wash oneself *lavar, lavarse*
washbasin *el lavabo*
wear, to wear *llevar*
weather *el tiempo*
week *la semana*
weekend *el fin de semana*
well *bien*
when *cuando*
where *donde*
which *que*
white *blanco*

who *quien, quienes*
why? *¿por qué?*
wife *la mujer, la señora*
wind *el viento*
window (kiosk, bank, etc.) *la ventanilla*
window (house) *la ventana*
wine *el vino*
winter *el invierno*
woman *la mujer*
word *la palabra*
work *el trabajo*
work, to work *trabajar*
write, to write *escribir*

year *el año*
yellow *amarillo*
yet t*odavía*
young *joven*

Subject index

Donde buscar ayuda   *Where to find help*

Here is a list of the key words and ideas in this book and the units where they are explained.

Congratulations! You have completed *Teach Yourself Beginner's Spanish* and are now a competent speaker of basic Spanish. You should be able to handle most everyday situations on a visit to Spain and to communicate with Spanish people sufficiently to make friends. If you would like to extend your ability so that you can develop your confidence, whether for social or business purposes, why not take your Spanish a step further with the full *Teach Yourself Spanish* or *Teach Yourself Business Spanish?*

SPANISH

Juan Kattán

A complete introductory course designed to help you achieve basic fluency in both spoken and written Spanish.

This book assumes that you have no previous knowledge of Spanish and takes you to the point at which you can read and write simple texts, and confidently take part in everyday conversations. The twenty–four units focus on communication in a whole host of practical situations and provide all the Spanish you need when travelling, shopping, ordering a meal and generally living in Spain. Each unit has lively dialogues which introduce useful vocabulary and grammar points, and exercises which test your understanding. You will also find a key to the exercises, a grammar index and a Spanish-English vocabulary list.

TEACH YOURSELF BOOKS

ESSENTIAL SPANISH GRAMMAR

Seymour Resnick

This book is designed specifically for those with limited learning time who want to be able to speak and understand simple, everyday Spanish. It is not condensed outline of Spanish grammar, teaching how to construct sentences from rules and vocabulary, but a series of aids and selected points of grammar enabling the student to use Spanish phrases and words more effectively and with greater versatility. Thus, although no previous knowledge of Spanish grammar is assumed, the student should be familiar with a number of phrases and expressions such as may be found in any phrase book.

The grammatical rules and forms, fundamental to the structure of the Spanish language, are presented in logical sequence, and they are all illustrated with useful phrases and sentences. There is a list of more than 2,500 words that are identical or nearly identical in form and meaning in English and Spanish, and a separate section on grammatical terms is also included.

TEACH YOURSELF BOOKS

BUSINESS SPANISH

Juan Kattán-Ibarra

A lively and easy-to-use introduction to spoken and written business Spanish.

This books starts with the basics and guides you quickly to confidence in using Spanish in a business context. Through a series of 24 graded units, you learn all the language skills that you will need when conducting business in Spain or Latin America, and at the same time you will pick up many useful tips on making appointments, arranging travel, applying for a job, buying and selling . . . there is something in this book for everyone.

Each of units 1–16 contain a dialogue, to help you develop your spoken Spanish, and examples and texts designed to build your understanding and confidence in written Spanish, in particular in the thorny area of commercial correspondence. Notes throw light on difficult points, and new grammar is explained with plenty of examples. You may test yourself with a series of exercises, with answers given in the back. Units 17–24 comprise passages in Spanish describing economic life in Spain and Latin America, which provide both good practice for the Spanish learnt in earlier units and a useful source of information. Finally, there is an extensive English – Spanish glossary of commercial terms, and a comprehensive Spanish – English vocabulary.

TEACH YOURSELF BOOKS